UNDERSTANDING
OPTIONS

Michael Sincere

McGraw-Hill

New York Chicago San Francisco Lisbon London
Madrid Mexico City Milan New Delhi
San Juan Seoul Singapore
Sydney Toronto

The *McGraw-Hill* Companies

3 4 5 6 7 8 9 0   DOC/DOC   0 9 8 7

ISBN-13: 978-0-07-147636-2
ISBN-10: 0-07-147636-9

This publication is designed to provide accurate and authoritative information in regard to the subject matter covered. It is sold with the understanding that neither the author nor the publisher is engaged in rendering legal, accounting, or other professional service. If legal advice or other expert assistance is required, the services of a competent professional person should be sought.
> —*From a declaration of principles jointly adopted by a committee of the American Bar Association and a committee of publishers.*

This book is printed on acid-free paper.

McGraw-Hill books are available at special quantity discounts to use as premiums and sales promotions, or for use in corporate training programs. For more information, please write to the Director of Special Sales, Professional Publishing, McGraw-Hill, Two Penn Plaza, New York, NY 10121-2298. Or contact your local bookstore.

Library of Congress Cataloging-in-Publication Data

Sincere, Michael.
    Understanding options / by Michael Sincere.
       p. cm.
    Includes index.
    ISBN 0-07-147636-9 (pbk. : alk. paper)
    1. Options (Finance) I. Title.
HG6024.A3.S562 2006
332.64'53—dc22   2006015646

*In memory of A. J., Roslyn, and Carolyn Gaines—
and my father, Charles, who will always be
remembered for his positive attitude and kindness.*

Contents

Acknowledgments

To the thousands of readers who bought my previous book, *Understanding Stocks*. Because of the success of this book, my editor, Stephen Isaacs at McGraw-Hill, decided to create an "Understanding" book series aimed at the novice investor and trader. This is the second book in the series, although many more are planned. I also want to thank Laura Libretti at McGraw-Hill for her wise advice about the publishing world. Finally, I want to thank Daina Penikas for her superb supervision of the editing process.

To my mother, Lois, for her help with editing and proofreading, and for always believing in me and my work.

To Howard Kornstein, a professional options trader, for sharing his extensive knowledge and expertise with me. He took the time to give insightful analysis of all the options strategies. Without his guidance and assistance, this book could not have been written.

To Mark D. Wolfinger, an ex-CBOE trader and author of *The Short Book on Options*, for his invaluable assistance in correcting errors. He is truly an options expert.

To Tom Reid, one of my favorite research consultants, whose work on this book was invaluable.

To Sylvia Coppersmith, for the support and guidance she provided our family.

To those who read the book and made suggestions for improvements, including Mike Fredericks, Joanne Pessin, Anthony Pike, and an extremely knowledgeable friend who thoroughly reviewed the book. He prefers to remain anonymous.

Once again, to the hardworking and pleasant staff at my favorite bookstore and cafe in Boca Raton, Florida, including Frenchy Maignan (who waited patiently for this book so he could begin trading), Jason Carnes, Victoria Correa, Sue Ercolino, Amanda Fuentes, Gina Fuentes, Tiffany Gearardo, Gloria Goldberg, Chris Granaghan, Greg Granaghan, Michael Harrison, Jenna Kellerhouse, Carlton Miller; Sarah Montes, Samuel Pohner, Jonathan Pollock, Colby Reifler, Nicole Vitale, and Eric Zabon.

And, finally, to my friends, family, and acquaintances: Idil Baran, Karina Benzine, Bruce Berger, Krystel Borg, Staci Capone, David Datny, Caitlyn DiJoseph, Angela Duque, Dave Eigen, Lourdes Fernandez-Vidal, Alice Fibigrova, Hanna Grigat, Elisa Gundersen, Tabitha Hunnewell, Christopher Johnson, Cindy Klassen, Jenny Langas, Marianne Larsen, Mariela Leon, Selina von Liel, Sanne Mueller, Frankie Misiano, Scott O'Connell, Jane Permanova, Anna Permanova, Tyrone Pike, Zdenka Piknova, Kenny Pineda, Anna Ridolfo, Karolina, Veronika, Jiri, and Jaroslava Roubickovi, Karina Royer, Joanna Rybka, Maria Schmidt, Luigi Silvestri, Alex Sincere, Miriam Sincere, Alexandra Slusarenko, Harvey Small, Oksana Smirnova, Bob and Brittany Spector, Lucie Stejskalova, Deron Wagner, Roland White, Jarle Wirgenes, Lene Wirgenes, and Jason Zimmer.

Preface

Who Should Read this Book

If you are thinking of trading stock options or you are already trading but losing money, this could be the most useful book you ever read. I have taken the classes, read the books, talked to the pros, and made the trades so I can teach you what I learned. Like my other books, I try to explain options as if you were sitting across from me at the kitchen table. My goal is to save you time and money while educating and entertaining you.

An options book that is entertaining? I know it sounds ridiculous, especially if you slogged through the dozens of other options books that are supposedly for beginners. Most of the options books I have read sound as though they were written for lawyers or mathematicians. They make options seem a lot more confusing than they actually are. Perhaps it's because options contracts are legal contracts that include specialized terms. As much as possible, I will leave most of the lawyerly talk out of this book.

I have one friend who is afraid to take risks and another one who is a speculator. When I told my timid friend he should consider trading options, he immediately snapped, "Are you crazy? That's way too complicated for me. I don't want to lose all my money." He was an experienced stock market investor who liked to buy and hold stocks and mutual funds. He believes that options are a get-rich-quick scheme that operates like a casino. He was convinced that options were not friendly to risk-averse investors.

My speculator friend, a successful dentist, is addicted to the Vegas-style action of the stock market. When the stock market wasn't exciting enough, he and his wife enrolled in an options seminar, plunking down $4,000 for the two-day course (not including the $2,000 software that supposedly chose winning options). The instructor pressed all the right buttons, and by the end of the class my friend was ready to plunge into options using sexy strategies like naked puts, bull and bear spreads, and straddles. He was convinced that he could quickly make a fortune in options through the most sophisticated strategies. He believed that the more complicated the strategy, the more money he'd make. Fortunately, he talked to me first.

I wrote this book for my two friends and thousands more like them. If you think that options are too complicated or dangerous, give me a chance to change your mind. The good news is that there is an options strategy that will meet the needs of both of my friends, from the risk-averse conservative investor to the risk-loving speculator. In addition, if you are reading this book not to make money but for education or entertainment, I believe the book will meet your needs.

If you are thinking of taking an expensive options course, then read this book first. It could save you thousands of dollars. Even if you still decide to take the course, you'll be much better prepared. Also, if you are one of the 10 million employees who receive stock options from your employer, this book could help you to understand the benefits and risks of stock options.

And, finally, if you are concerned this book is too basic, there are enough advanced strategies in later chapters to whet your appetite, including a dynamic interview with an options guru. I describe all of the advanced strategies with my usual reader-friendly style.

What's So Great about Options?

What if I told you that you could use options to make money every month or every quarter? And what if I told you that you can use options as insurance, for example, to protect your stock portfolio? And if, on occasion, you wanted to speculate, you could leverage your money to double or triple your profits. It will cost you a lot less than if you bought stocks. And, finally, if you like to short stocks, it is safer to use options strategies than to use the stock market.

Speaking of safety, did you know the single best reason for choosing options is that you know in advance how much you can lose? You are in control of how much risk you are willing to take. If used properly, options can be used by all investors or traders to generate income, for insurance, and to speculate. By the time you finish this book, you should have a good idea what options can do for you and whether you want to participate.

For example, one of my friends who just started trading called to tell me he experimented with a sophisticated options strategy called a *straddle* (explained later in this book). After investing $2,000, he sold the option for a $25,000 profit the next day. Perhaps it was beginner's luck, but it goes to show you can hit a home run on occasion. Another friend has been using a conservative options strategy called *selling covered calls* to receive monthly income.

One reason you'll like options is that you can make money no matter what the market conditions. That doesn't include all the advanced strategies, which will be discussed in detail throughout the book. Options are a powerful tool that, if used properly, can be used in conjunction with the stock market to enhance your portfolio.

At the very least, it's smart to learn everything you can about this fascinating and flexible financial instrument. When you hear that options are flexible, it simply means that you can trade them under any market condition and that the strategies can be as simple or as complicated as you want to make them. Can you think of any other financial instrument besides stocks that meets the needs of investors no matter what their income level or financial goals?

How the Book Is Organized

This book is divided into six parts. Part One, "What You Need to Know First," includes a thorough overview of options. Beginning with Part Two, the book is organized the same way as you would trade, from introductory Level 1 strategies to advanced Level 4 strategies. After you gain more experience, you may want to take a closer look at the advanced strategies. In addition, you'll enjoy the must-read interview with Sheldon Natenberg, best-selling author and a recognized options expert. And finally, in the last section, a list of books, classes, software, and other resources are included for those who want to continue studying options. (If you have questions while reading this book, I include a toll-free phone number in Chapter 18 that will give you immediate answers.)

Some of you might wonder how it's possible to write such a short book when most options books are well over 500 pages. First, most of those books are aimed at the pros, not retail traders. Second, other authors devote hundreds of pages to explaining how options are constructed using complicated formulas. Although I do introduce pricing formulas, my theory is you don't have to learn how an engine works to drive a car.

Although analyzing options formulas might be interesting to mathematicians, I'd prefer to keep my eye on the bottom line, which is to teach you what you need to know to successfully trade options. Trading options is not as hard as many people think, but it's also not as easy as some want you to believe.

How to Contact Me

It is estimated that only 5 percent of the population actually understands how options work. It's easy to understand why. After all, it takes skill, knowledge, experience, and perseverance to be a successful options trader. By the time you finish the book, perhaps you can join this small group of knowledgeable traders.

Thank you in advance for taking the time to read my book. You may have to read it a few times before you truly understand options, but I think it will be worth it to you. And, finally, if you have questions about my book or notice any errors, feel free to e-mail me at msincere@gmail.com or visit my Web site, www.michaelsincere.com. I always enjoy hearing from you.

PART ONE

WHAT YOU NEED TO KNOW FIRST

1

Welcome to the Options Market

I'm delighted that you decided to join me as we learn more about options and options trading. If this is your first time, options might seem confusing, at least at first. Options can be deceiving, as if you are walking through quicksand. At the beginning, it seems straightforward and easy. But as you get in deeper, it can get murkier, and before long you find yourself sinking under the weight of options terminology.

As you become more familiar with the strategies, it gets easier. But don't get me wrong. Learning about options is like learning a new language. The good news is that you don't need an advanced degree in mathematics to be a successful options trader. In fact, all you need is a computer and a calculator. If you need to do sophisticated calculations, most brokerage firms have software programs that can provide you with quick answers.

As usual, the best way to learn is in small steps, which is exactly how I present the information. If you are like my speculator friends, you will want to jump right into options strategies. But I urge you to take the time to first understand the purpose and uses of options. There is always time to learn about the strategies (starting in Part Two).

Suggestion: Before you trade options, it's essential that you have a working knowledge of the stock market. Because stocks and options are linked (some would say they feed off of each other), you should know how to invest in stocks before you can trade options. If you are new to the stock market, I recommend my previous book, *Understanding Stocks* (McGraw-Hill, 2003), which quickly and easily covers what you need to know about the stock market. There are many other books on this subject at your local bookstore.

The Advantages of Trading Options

Before we discuss options in detail, let's take a closer look at the reasons you'd want to participate in them. Did you know that options were created thousands of years ago? And they were popular well before the first stock market was created. You also might be surprised to learn that options can be included in anyone's portfolio, from conservative, risk-averse investors to speculators. Many traders love trading options because of their flexibility and low cost. No matter what your reason, you can find a way to use options—for income, for insurance, or for speculation.

Income

I'll discuss income strategies thoroughly in Part Two, but for now remember that options can be used quite effectively to generate income or cash flow. Basically, instead of buying options, you sell options on stocks that you already own. In a way, you are renting your stocks to other people, and they pay you for the privilege. This can be a profitable way to use options, similar to an annuity where you can receive cash each month just for holding the stocks.

Insurance

Another effective use of options is to hedge or insure your invest-ments. Let's say you have a rather large position in one stock. If you prefer to reduce risk, you can use options to insure or hedge your stock position in case of disaster. Originally, options were created for just this purpose.

Speculation

Some speculators have caused options to have a reputation as a "get-rich-quick" casino. For very little up-front money, you can leverage your investments to make many times more than you put in. With this strategy, you are controlling a lot of shares of stock for a little bit of money. There are also strategies that allow traders with little money to make a lot of money. The best part of these options strategies is that you usually know in advance how much you could lose.

Myth versus Truth

Perhaps you believe that the only people making money in options are those who use the more advanced strategies. This isn't true! For the retail options trader, sometimes the simpler the strategy, the more money you'll make. And the more complicated the strategy, the more risk you take. Just stick with strategies that you are comfortable with—the ones that don't keep you up at night. This pertains to the stock market as well as to options.

More than likely, it's too early for you to know the best way to use options. Many options traders use a combination of strategies: they employ options for income or cash flow and also for hedging against potential disasters. Obviously, many people are attracted to options because they can make many times their initial investment.

Buying an Option on a House

This short story should give you a general understanding of how options work.

Let's say you are thinking of buying a particular two-bedroom house that is listed for $100,000. You really like this house and think the price is fair. You are eager to lock in the price at $100,000 in case it does go higher. If you can lock in the price, you'll have time to look at other houses and also time to act quickly if you decide to buy.

So you approach the owner of the house to see if she will sign an options agreement. When she agrees, you sit down to discuss the terms. After a short conversation, the owner of the house agrees to hold the house for you for three months. During this time, no one else will be allowed to buy it. It also means that no matter how high or how low other offers may be for the house, you will be allowed to buy it for $100,000. Even if a realtor puts the house on the market for $120,000 within the next three months, you, and only you, are allowed to buy it for $100,000. The owner still pays the bills but you control when, if, and for how much the house will be sold. What a great deal.

But what if the house goes down in value to $90,000, for example? According to the rules of the options contract you signed, you can just walk away if you want. In lawyer talk, you have the "right" to buy the house for $100,000, but you are not "obligated" to buy it. That means no matter how much the house is worth, higher or lower, you can buy the house for $100,000 or choose to walk away from the deal. (By the way, you will hear the word *right*, a lot, because options give you the right to buy or sell.)

Perhaps you're thinking, "What does the owner get out of this transaction?" That's a good question. Because the owner is holding the house for you and can't let anyone else buy it, she will want some compensation; that is, she wants money. Typically, the owner will want a small percentage of the purchase price, perhaps 2 percent, or $2,000. So for $2,000, she will hold the house for you for three months. (By the way, the $2,000 you pay the owner is called the *premium*.)

The owner is pleased because she gets $2,000 from you, which she can use as she pleases. You're happy because for three months you know you won't have to pay more than $100,000 for the house. In your opinion, $2,000 is a small price to pay for the right to hold this house. And if you change your mind during the next three months, although you will lose the money you paid the owner, you are free to look for another house.

Let's see what could happen in real life. If the value of the house zooms up to $120,000, you decide to buy the house for $100,000 as previously agreed. Guess what? You just made a $20,000 paper profit.

If you changed your mind or the price of the house dropped below $100,000, you aren't obligated or forced to buy it. You walk away from the deal with a $2,000 loss, but it's better than buying a house that has dropped in value.

But what about the owner? She doesn't care if you buy the house; she's happy to receive the $2,000. And when the three months are up, if you don't buy the house, she could write another options agreement with someone else. This way she can continue getting these tidy little premium checks from potential buyers.

Buying Options on Snow Shovels in Chicago

To give you another example of how people use options in the real world, I have another story. Let's say that you own a hardware store in Chicago. You know that you'll probably need snow shovels in December. After all, last year there was a huge December snowstorm. Within weeks, you ran out of snow shovels, costing you profits and annoying your customers. This year, in August, you arrange an options agreement with the snow shovel manufacturer, Shovels, Inc.

The options agreement specifies that Shovels, Inc., will provide you with 100 snow shovels for $15 each, although it normally charges much more. The options agreement specifies that you have the right to buy the snow shovels for $15 each until the third Friday in December. You don't have to buy the shovels, but you can if you want to.

If it doesn't snow by the third Friday in December, you probably won't buy the snow shovels. Remember the premium in the first story? The manufacturer will charge you a $300 premium for holding the 100 snow shovels at $15 each. No matter what happens, whether you take delivery of the snow shovels or not, you will lose the $300.

Why would Shovels, Inc., sell you an option on snow shovels? First, the company receives the $300 premium from you. Second, the company knows there is a chance you could buy the snow shovels, so an option to buy is better than nothing.

Let's see what happens in the real world. If there is a brutal snowstorm in November and everyone needs snow shovels, the price of shovels will go up. You are delighted because you have the right to buy the snow shovels for $15 each. You accept delivery of the snow shovels and sell them to your customers for an even higher price. That will be very profitable for you.

Let's say the Chicago winter turns out to be very mild. In this case, you don't want the snow shovels at all. You don't accept delivery of the shovels and the options contract expires. In this worst-case scenario you lost the $300, but at least you aren't stuck with the delivery of 100 unneeded snow shovels. In a way, the options contract was an insurance policy.

If it's a mild winter, Shovels, Inc., keeps your $300 and the 100 snow shovels. In fact, the company will wait until January and sell an option on the 100 snow shovels to someone else. The money the manufacturer receives for each options contract will help it get through the mild winter.

You might not realize it, but options contracts are written on thousands of products, from corn, soybeans, and oil to houses, snow shovels, and stocks.

A Very Important Question

Think about the following question: Would you rather be the options buyer or the options seller? The buyer is in control of when the property or product is bought or sold. But the seller receives the premium and must follow the terms of the contract. As we examine stock options further, you will learn strategies for both buyers and sellers. Meanwhile, think about which you'd rather be: the options buyer or the options seller.

The Early Years

The Bible has the first recorded option transaction (the book of Genesis), involving a marriage agreement between Jacob and one of Laban's daughters, Rachel. The date of this transaction is estimated to be about 1700 B.C. Under the terms of this option agreement, Jacob had the "right" to marry Rachel but only if he agreed to seven years of labor. Apparently, Laban changed the terms of the agreement and insisted that Jacob marry his older daughter instead. Jacob was so determined to marry Rachel that he took out another option agreement for another seven years of labor. Finally, after fulfilling the terms of the contract, Jacob was allowed to marry Rachel.

Many years later, Aristotle (384–322 BC) wrote a story about Thales of Miletus, a poor Greek astronomer, mathematician, and philosopher, which is the first written record of option speculation.

According to Aristotle, Thales studied the stars to make unusually accurate predictions about future weather conditions, coming to the conclusion that the olive crop would be "bountiful," in other words, have an excellent season in the fall. Thales was clever enough to take advantage of his prediction. Although he didn't have a lot of money, he quietly approached the owners of the olive presses (the presses were used to convert olives into olive oil) to make an offer.

He paid each owner a deposit (or premium) to reserve the olive presses during the harvest. For a small deposit, the owners would hold or reserve the olive presses for Thales during the autumn. Because no one believed that Thales could predict the weather nine months in the future, no one bid against him. Therefore, Thales paid very little for the right to reserve the olive presses.

As it turned out, Thales's prediction was correct. It was an excellent year for olives and the demand for the olive presses was enormous. Thales sold his options contract (which was the right to use the olive presses) to the owners for a huge profit.

The moral of the story: Thales proved to the world (and himself) that philosophers or speculators can become rich if they are clever enough to figure out how to use options in the real world. (It also helps to do your research before you invest.)

Eighteenth Century

The first options market in the United States began in 1791, when the New York Stock Exchange (NYSE) opened. Because options were still not considered part of the regular market, transactions were arranged in the less prestigious "over-the-counter" market. Options buyers and sellers had to walk around the floor looking for a match. Obviously, it wasn't easy to match buyers and sellers, especially before computers and telephones. There was no central place that buyers and sellers could meet to trade options. One of the ways buyers and sellers would meet was through newspaper ads placed by firms who had options they wanted to buy or sell.

Nineteenth Century

By the turn of the century, stock options were traded through a loose organization of over-the-counter dealers known as the Put and Call Brokers and Dealers Association. One of the problems was that no one knew what was considered a fair price for an option. Therefore, it was quite easy to make a bad deal and lose money. In addition, because no one guaranteed the options contract, traders were basically on their own. Finally, negotiating an option contract was difficult because the terms for each contract were unique. Unfortunately, traders had to wait another 100 years before the first organized options exchange was created.

================================

· ·

Now that you have a general idea of how to use options, in the next chapter you'll learn how to open up an options account.

C H A P T E R

How to Open an Options Account

The two most common questions that people ask when interested in options are "How do you open an account?" and "How much money do I need to get started?" Both questions will be answered in this short but important chapter.

By now, you may be anxious to place your first options trade. The best traders, however, wait patiently for the best investment or trading opportunities. If you step into options without knowledge or experience, you could lose money. Take the time to study options thoroughly before you place your first order. With that in mind, let's get started on learning what you need to do to open an account.

The Five Steps to Opening an Options Account

Because your brokerage firm handles all your options trades, you must begin with a brokerage account. After you have opened your brokerage account, you are then ready to open an options account. You can fill out the forms on the Internet or have them mailed to you. Once again, you must have at least a basic knowledge of the stock market to successfully trade options.

After you've opened your brokerage account with the required minimum (the exact dollar amount varies with each brokerage firm but typically you'll need a minimum of $2,500), the brokerage firm will determine how much money you need to open an options account. Again, the exact amount varies from firm to firm.

Step One: The Brokerage Firm

In the old days, you had to rely on a stockbroker to make an options trade for you, but you paid dearly for the privilege. Because of the Internet, it's almost required that you make your own trades. This is one of the reasons why options commissions have dropped so dramatically, to as little as $10 a trade (or lower) in recent years.

Nevertheless, when you first get started with options, there is nothing wrong with having the brokerage firm representative place the trade for you or at least confirm the trades that you make. (It will cost a little more if the representative makes the trade.)

Although you should consider the expense of commissions when choosing an online brokerage firm, you also want knowledgeable representatives (they are no longer called stockbrokers), who will help guide you through the trades and discuss basic and advanced strategies. You also want a brokerage firm that has sophisticated options software and tools that can route your trades quickly to the best bid and ask price. In addition, you want access to educational materials like online tutorials and articles. It is also helpful if the reps are available to answer questions for you at least 12 hours a day.

Choose the brokerage firm that offers all of the above. If you stick with well-known brokerage firms, they have options professionals willing and eager to help you set up and manage your options account.

Step Two: The Margin Agreement

If you borrow money from a broker to purchase stocks, you are "buying on margin" and need to open a margin account.

If you do decide to open a margin account at your brokerage, you will first have to fill out a margin agreement for your brokerage account, which is similar to making a credit application. The brokerage firm will run a credit check on you and require you to truthfully fill out a detailed questionnaire. The brokerage firm wants to make sure you have the financial resources and knowledge to handle margin. It also wants you to understand the possible risks. If your credit is good, you should have no problem getting the application approved.

Margin is similar to a credit card. You don't have to use it; in fact, most people would be wise not to buy stocks on margin, but you can. Nevertheless, there are times when traders might need to use margin to buy stocks. A lot of people don't realize that by signing a margin agreement, they are also allowing the brokerage firm to lend their stocks to others. You should know that most people with brokerage accounts do tend to open up margin accounts rather than a cash account.

If you are using Level 1 and Level 2 option strategies (explained below), you will *not* need to fill out a margin agreement. After all, options are not "marginable" and must be paid in full. On the other hand, if you want to do more advanced options trading, it is required that you have a margin account. (This will make more sense when you read about advanced options strategies.)

If you are a new trader, it's not necessary (or even recommended) that you open up a margin account. Because it's so easy to get into trouble using margin, it's probably best to avoid borrowing from your brokerage until you gain a lot more trading experience.

Another interesting fact: Margin agreements are not usually allowed on an IRA, a tax-deferred 401(k), or a trust account (you are required to have what is called a *cash account*). However, some firms do allow it. Nevertheless, you are still allowed to have an options account in your IRA or tax-deferred account. The only catch is that you will be limited to using basic options strategies. Later on, you'll learn this isn't necessarily a disadvantage. Best advice: Check with your brokerage firm for the specific rules regarding margin.

Step Three: The Options Agreement

The options agreement must be completed if you want to trade options. The purpose of the options agreement is that the brokerage firm wants to determine how much knowledge and experience you have. (After you've read this book, you will have no problem with the options agreement.) The brokerage firm wants to know that you fully understand the risks of trading options and that you have the financial ability to take care of any losses. It will ask you questions about your net worth, your bank, your employer, your experience and knowledge with trading stocks and options, and how much risk you are willing to take.

If you have never traded options before, you will only be approved for Level 1 and Level 2 options trading. Before I tell you why, let's go over the options trading levels.

- Level 1 Options Trading: Selling Covered Calls
- Level 2 Options Trading: Buying Calls and Puts
- Level 3 Options Trading: Straddles, Spreads, and the Strangle
- Level 4 Options Trading: Selling Naked Puts and Calls
- Level 5 Options Trading: Selling Naked Indexes

As I mentioned above, the brokerage firm will be very cautious about approving a newcomer for anything higher than Level 2. After all, if you got involved in professional-level trading strategies and lost your entire investment, guess who would get stuck paying the bill? The brokerage firm could be liable for the loss.

At the end of the agreement, you have to sign and date the form. I don't know why, but most people sign even though they don't read the agreements thoroughly. You must read this form before signing (and that includes any contracts you have to sign).

Step Four: The Brochure

Every brokerage firm is required to give you a copy of this tedious but technical brochure *Characteristics and Risks of Standardized Options* (also called the *options disclosure document*). It's not an easy read, but it is filled with useful information and calculations. I have a feeling that although everyone agrees to read this brochure, few really do. Nevertheless, if you read the brochure carefully, you will learn all the risks of trading options. After you read about all the potential risks, you might change your mind about trading options!

Suggestion: I strongly suggest that you first read this entire book before you read the brochure *Characteristics and Risks of Standardized Options*. After reading this book, the brochure will make a lot more sense.

Step Five: The Standardized Options Contract

All options contracts are standardized, which means that the terms of the option are the same for all people. In the old days, options contracts were created on a case-by-case or individual basis, so it was every person for him- or herself. That is one of the reasons why options got such a bad name. As soon as they standardized the terms of the agreement, then it was a level playing field.

By the way, when you buy or sell an option, it is a legal contract, so you must fulfill the terms of the contract. That is another reason why it's so important you fully understand what you are getting involved in when you buy and sell contracts.

A Tarnished Reputation

As I wrote in my previous book *Understanding Stocks*, one of the most fascinating bubbles in history occurred in Holland in the seventeenth century. In 1635, people were willing to pay nearly any amount of money to own a single tulip bulb. These bulbs became status symbols for the rich and famous. Some of the bulbs were beautiful mutations, what the Dutch called *bizarres*. Speculators would buy one, then immediately sell it for a higher price.

As the tulip mania increased, speculators pushed the prices of tulips even higher. For example, to buy one exotic tulip bulb, you would have had to exchange several horses, pigs, bread, a carriage, tons of cheese, beer, and house furnishings (using today's exchange rate, well over $200,000).

The entire country got swept up in the tulip mania. As with most bubbles, people don't know they're in one until it is too late. At the time, people thought the tulips were wise investments that would last forever. Many investors were more than willing to trade their houses or valuable paintings for one tulip bulb.

So what does this have to do with options? Some speculators, to juice up their returns, bought options on the tulip bulbs, which also allowed those who couldn't afford to participate in the regular market to speculate in options.

As the price of the options climbed, the speculators would turn around and sell them for even higher prices. Some people made fortunes without ever taking possession of the tulips. It was not uncommon for people to make a 20-fold profit on their tulip bulb options, turning a $1,000 investment into a $20,000 windfall a few months later. In addition, some tulip dealers bought put options (called *time bargains*) as a hedge in case the tulip prices dropped.

The tulip bubble popped rather dramatically and abruptly. Suddenly, the outrageous prices of tulip bulbs began to plunge. People looked around and wondered how anyone could pay that much for an exotic flower. People who only a few months before hadn't been able to buy the tulip bulbs fast enough now couldn't sell them in time. The Dutch government promised to pay 10 percent of the price of the tulips, but by then it was too late.

When the tulip market crashed, many speculators were unable to honor their original option agreements. Many owed more money on their options than they originally invested. Family fortunes were wiped out, there was widespread panic, and the Dutch economy collapsed. Some blamed the use and misuse of options as the main culprit for the crash. In retrospect, it was obvious that people were unaware of the risks of speculating in options. As a result of this incident, Europeans had a negative view of options trading, and options were declared illegal in some European countries.

Brief History of Options in the United States
In the United States, options were also used in several schemes that were designed to take advantage of investors' lack of knowledge. At the time, there was little or no regulation. According to the book *Options* (McGraw-Hill, 1999) by The Options Institute, brokers would recommend undesirable stocks to unsuspecting clients.

For participating in this scheme, options speculators would reward stockbrokers with large quantities of call options.

As more and more clients bought the underlying stock, both the options and underlying stock would rise in price. As is typical of these kinds of "pump-and-dump" schemes, the speculators and stockbrokers sold their options and stock, while the clients were left holding the now worthless stock.

Another scheme involved creating an "option pool." Major stockholders would buy large amounts of options in an underlying stock. The options allowed them to manipulate and control the price of the stock. As a result, the price of the option would rise or fall based on rumors of what the option pools were buying or selling rather than on the financial expectations of the company.

After the stock market crashed in 1929, many of these schemes were exposed. At first, an angry Congress outlawed options completely as many investors lost everything. During the investigation phase of the stock market crash, the options industry sent an experienced trader and representative, Herbert Filer, to testify in front of Congress.

Filer explained to a confused Congress that options were similar to insurance contracts to protect against market volatility. At the time, although most options were worthless when they expired, buying options was similar to paying an insurance premium on your house. "If you insured your house against fire and it didn't burn down, you would not say you had thrown away your insurance premium," he testified. (For further explanation, see *Options*, McGraw-Hill, 1999.)

As a result of Filer's convincing arguments, Congress agreed that not all options trading was manipulated and, in fact, could be a valuable tool if used properly. The Investment Act of 1934 legalized options and in 1935 the newly formed Securities and Exchange Commission (SEC) granted the Chicago Board of Trade (CBOT) a license to register the options market as a securities exchange. The Securities and Exchange Commission continues to regulate the options industry to this day. Ironically, the CBOT didn't actually take advantage of this license and register as an options exchange until 1968.

. . . .

Now that you've learned how to open an options account, you're going to learn about the fascinating characteristics of options.

3

The Fascinating Characteristics of Options

Remember when I said that learning about options is like learning a new language? You'll understand what I mean when you read this important chapter. Think of it this way. What if you had never seen or driven an automobile but read everything you could about the steering wheel? No matter how much you read about this important and powerful device, you wouldn't know what it was like to use a steering wheel until you started driving. Learning about options is similar.

In this chapter, you'll discover that options really do have their own special language that will seem unusual, at least at first. After you master the options language and start trading, it will all begin to make sense. So get ready for a unique experience as I introduce to you the fascinating characteristics of an extremely flexible and powerful financial instrument, the stock option.

The Official Definition of Stock Options

The official definition from one of the options exchanges, is rather technical. A *stock option* is "a contract that gives the owner the right, but not the obligation, to buy or sell a particular asset (the underlying stock) at a fixed price (the strike price) for a specific period of time (until expiration). The contract also obligates the writer to meet the terms of delivery if the contract right is exercised by the owner."

No wonder people think that options are complicated. A simpler definition would be that a stock option is "the right to buy or sell a specific stock at a certain price for a limited period of time." This is a much better definition, but if you are still confused, don't worry. By the time you finish this chapter, you will have a pretty good idea of what options are all about.

The Official Definition of Stock Options Explained

You already know that stock options are contracts. Remember the stories about the house and the snow shovels? You had the right to buy the house, but you didn't have to. In other words, you had the right but not the obligation to buy the house. It was the same with the snow shovels. According to the options contract, you had the right to buy the snow shovels but you weren't obligated, or forced, to. You could walk away from the contract at any time.

Stock options are very similar. For example, an options contract gives you the right to buy a stock but you are not required to do so. Unlike a share of stock, which is ownership of something real, an options contract is intangible.

This will make more sense if you allow me to tell one more story.

A Story about Stock Options

Let's say you are interested in a stock—Tracking, Inc.—that you think is going up. It is currently trading for $10 a share. You are sure it's going a lot higher within a few months. So you decide to buy an options contract.

According to the options contract, you have the right to buy 100 shares of Tracking, Inc., for $10 a share anytime within the next three months. If Tracking, Inc., moves higher, to $11, $12, or even $15, you can still buy shares of Tracking, Inc., for $10 each. What if you are wrong and Tracking, Inc., goes down in price? In fact, if Tracking, Inc., is lower than $10 by the time the options contract expires, you definitely don't want to buy it anymore. You will only buy it if it's $10 or higher anytime within the next three months. Just as with the house and the snow shovels, it seems to be a very good deal. The stockholder still owns Tracking, Inc., but you control the shares.

So what does the real seller of the option get? He receives money from you. Do you remember the name of the money that the owner receives? (In case you forgot, it's called the *premium*.) In the case of this stock option, the premium is rather cheap, perhaps no more than $100.

Basically, for only $100 you have the right to buy 100 shares of Tracking, Inc., for $10 a share within the next three months. You are not obligated to buy it, but you can. If you had bought stock instead of options, it would have cost you a lot more.

Let's see what happens in real life: Tracking, Inc., suddenly announces that it is developing a new product, a GPS tracking device, and the stock zooms higher. In one day Tracking, Inc., went from $10 a share to $18 a share. Excellent! According to the options contract, you can buy Tracking, Inc., for $10 a share even though it's actually worth $18. That's an $800 paper profit.

And here's the interesting part. The premium on the stock option was $100 when the stock was selling for $10 a share. Now that the stock is selling for $18 a share, the premium went up a lot. The owner of Tracking, Inc., is satisfied because he gets to keep the $100 premium, although he might be kicking himself a little for selling the option to you so cheaply.

You also have another choice, which is what makes options so fascinating. As the option buyer, you can also turn around and sell the options contract to someone else for $900. If you do this, you don't have to go through the trouble of buying the stock. In just a few weeks, you made an $800 profit without ever owning the stock.

Perhaps you think it's impossible to make money this quickly. Although it's not easy, it's quite possible. I have a friend who made over $130,000 in three days buying options in a biomedical company. He had read that the company might get approved for a new drug. Just on the rumor alone, the options went up over 400 percent. (Later in the book, I'll tell you what happened to his money.)

The Unique Characteristics of Options

Now that you have a general idea of how options work, let's look at some very unusual characteristics of options. Remember what I said. Sometimes the deeper you dig, the more confusing it gets. But to truly understand options, you have to learn their very specialized language. Although I can guarantee the next section will be educational, it will be a challenge to make it entertaining. I promise, however, to do my best.

Options have unique characteristics that are very important to understand. After we discuss these characteristics, I'll put all the pieces together and show you how they work together as a finely tuned financial instrument.

The Underlying Stock: "Without me, you're nothing!"

Without the underlying stock, there would be no options contract. Many people underestimate the importance of the underlying stock. In fact, one of the keys to success in the options market is choosing the correct underlying stock.

By itself, an option isn't worth anything. If you think about it, stock options are only paper contracts that give you the right to buy or sell a stock. Think of it this way. Every option is linked or attached to a stock, which is called the *underlying stock*. (Another definition for options is "derivative," which means that options are derived, or based on, another financial instrument. In the case of stock options, it is derived from a stock.)

You might wonder which stocks are allowed to have options. Actually, there are exchange-written options on more than 2,500 stocks trading on six options exchanges. The most well-known stocks have options, for example, General Electric, IBM, Apple, Microsoft, Home Depot, to name only a few. The six participant exchanges that allow options trading have very strict rules governing which stocks are allowed to have options.

Penny stocks, that is, stocks that trade for under $3 a share, are not allowed to have options. Generally, if you stick with well-known companies, you should get a lot of trading opportunities. You know from the stock market that when you trade stocks that are under $3 a share, there isn't a lot of liquidity. It's the same with options.

There is something else you should know about an underlying stock. Although I casually mentioned it earlier, you need to pay attention now because this is important. The following formula illustrates how options and stocks are linked.

1 standard options contract = 100 shares of stock

You can see from the formula that an options contract and the underlying stock are related. This is important when calculating what you are paying or receiving. To be technical, one standard options contract gives you the "rights" on 100 shares of stock.

Therefore, if you bought or sold two contracts, that would be equal to 200 shares. Five contracts equal 500 shares. If you bought or sold 10 contracts, that would be equal to buying 1,000 shares of a stock. Always remember to use 100 as a multiplier when calculating how many options to buy or sell.

One mistake that many beginners make is confusing contracts and shares. So when it comes time to enter the options order, instead of entering one contract, they become mixed up and enter 100 contracts. Do you realize what that means? They just bought the rights to buy or sell 10,000 shares of the underlying stock! I'll do my best to make sure you don't make that mistake when we discuss order entries.

When you are first starting out, you will practice by trading only one options contract (or 100 shares). That way, if something goes wrong, you won't lose very much. It's a small price to pay to gain experience.

The Secret of Options Is Revealed

There is something else you should know about an option's underlying stock. When the underlying stock goes up in price, so does the option. Now you know the secret of options. In other words, if you pick a profitable underlying stock, your option will usually go up in value. If the stock goes up high enough, eventually the stock and option will move together on a one-to-one basis. This is as sweet as it gets for an options buyer.

No matter whether you are an options buyer or seller, the key to success in options is choosing the right underlying stock. Where the stock goes, the option follows. And that is the secret of options that many people forget.

The Expiration Date

At the stroke of midnight on Saturday following the third Friday of the month, I disappear forever.

Another unique characteristic about options is that they always expire. After a certain date and time, called the *expiration date*, options are nothing but a worthless piece of paper. Some people call them wasting assets because over time they no longer exist. As soon as you buy or sell an options contract, the clock begins ticking. Think of a scuba diver who only has a certain amount of air left in her tank.

The expiration date is listed on every options contract. What is the expiration date? It's officially 11:59 p.m. on the Saturday after the third Friday of each month. In other words, all contracts cease trading on the third Friday of each month at 4 p.m. ET, which is when the market closes. If you pay attention to the stock market, you'll notice that the television commentators refer to it as "options expiration day."

Another interesting fact is that the third Friday of each quarter, when thousands of options contracts expire simultaneously, is referred to as "triple (or quadruple) witching day." On this day, the stock market is often volatile.

Unlike stocks, which exist indefinitely (unless a company goes out of business or merges), every options contract expires, sometimes in a month, sometimes longer. By the way, because all options eventually expire, they can be a bit riskier than stocks. It's the time pressure that makes them riskier. Because you know in advance that the option will expire in a few months, you have to make your profits quickly. In Part Two I will discuss how to use this time pressure to your advantage.

An expiration date secret: The more time that is left on an options contract, the more valuable the contract.

Type: Call-Put-Buy-Sell (That's All You Have to Know)

Believe it or not, there are only two types of options: a *call* and a *put*. And with these two types of options, you can take only two actions: buy or sell. That's correct. Every option strategy is based on buying or selling calls or puts. Although there are dozens of fancy-sounding options strategies, all are based on buying or selling calls or puts. Call-Put-Buy-Sell—don't forget these four words.

Although this entire book is devoted to buying or selling calls or puts, here is a brief description to get you started.

Call

A call option is similar to "going long" a stock (it means you believe the stock will rise) If you believe that the underlying stock will go up in price, you would buy a call. Remember the options secret? If the underlying stock goes up in price, the call option usually follows. The attractive part about call options is that you can "synthetically" participate in the upswing of a stock without actually owning the stock—and for a lot less money.

Put

A put option usually refers to shorting a stock (it means you believe the stock will fall). In other words, if you believe that the underlying stock will go down in price, or you want to protect your stock from a downward move, you will buy a put. Many people are so confused about shorting stocks that I have discussed this in detail in Part Four, "How to Buy Puts." Keep in mind that if the underlying stock goes down in price, the put option usually goes up. One huge advantage of buying a put option is that it's less risky than shorting—and less expensive.

The Strike Price: The Fixed Target Price

In option terminology, the predetermined, or fixed, price of a stock option is the *strike price*. Believe me, the strike price is a very important piece of information, which you'll discover when you first start trading. You already know how stocks and options are related to each other. One way to define the strike price is to think of it as a target price. It's the target price of the underlying stock.

Remember, when you buy an option you are actually buying the right to buy or sell an underlying stock at a certain price—the strike price. This is the price at which you have the right to buy or sell the stock. It is also the price that you want the stock to reach before the option expires.

To help you understand the strike price, let's review our examples. Remember when you bought an option on the house to buy it for $100,000. The strike price was $100,000 (although you hoped the price of the house would go higher). And remember when you bought the snow shovels at a fixed price of $15, no matter how high the shovels went up? The strike price was $15. And remember when you were willing to buy the stock in Tracking, Inc., for $10 a share? The strike price was $10 (although you wanted the stock price to go higher).

By itself, the strike price has no value. To use an analogy, you could say the strike price is like a series of steps on a staircase that moves in increments of $5 or $10. You have your choice of many different strike prices.

For example, although Tracking, Inc., is currently trading for $10 a share, you can choose strike prices from $5 all the way up to $25 (in the case of this stock, the strike price moves in $5 increments).

First Advanced Hint: If you choose a high strike price of $25, you must be brave or know something others don't know. This means that by the time the option expires in a few months, you expect Tracking, Inc., to reach at least $25 a share. If you're right, you'll make a fortune. If you're wrong, well, you lose what you invested.

Second Advanced Hint: Perhaps you have already noticed that the higher the strike price, the less the option will cost. If a stock is trading at $10 a share and you choose a $10 strike price, it will be costly. A $12 strike price may cost less. A $15 strike price could be cheap. A $20 strike price may cost you pennies.

Third Advanced Hint: A high strike price combined with a distant expiration date equals a very cheap option.

Final Hint: Don't forget the strike price. That is how you'll know if you're profitable or not.

The Premium = The Price

As you know by now, the *premium* is extremely important to options traders. If you are a buyer, it is the price you pay for an option. If you are a seller, it is the price you receive. Just as in an auction, the premium constantly changes. It goes up and down based on the supply and demand of the market. If you are experienced with the stock market, you will recognize the premium as the *bid* and *ask* price. Technically, the premium could also be a price *between* the bid and ask price. Think of the premium as the price you paid or received for the contract.

Still Confused by Options?

Until you actually start trading, understanding some of these concepts can be difficult. As soon as you start trading options in the next section, the concepts will make a lot more sense.

But if you are still confused by option terminology, maybe this weather analogy will help. Options traders love weather analogies.

What is the probability that in July it will be 80 degrees in Chicago? What is the probability that it will be 100 degrees? What is the probability it will be 75 degrees? The strike prices are like the temperature, ranging from 70 to 100 degrees in increments of 5 degrees (70 degrees, 75 degrees, 80 degrees, etc.).

The probability that the temperature in Chicago will reach at least 75 degrees in July is very good, so the cost of this contract will be rather high. The probability of the temperature in Chicago reaching at least 100 degrees in July is a long shot—possible, but not likely. The cost of this contract will be very low.

Next July, if the temperature reaches 75 degrees in Chicago, the cost of the 75 degree strike price will be quite valuable. On the other hand, the 100 degree strike price will be nearly worthless. And if it really reaches 100 degrees in July in Chicago, the 100 degree strike price will be extremely valuable (perhaps five times more valuable than the 75 degree strike price).

I hope this analogy helped you to understand options. Many people need hands-on experience with trading options before they fully understand how they work (beginning with the next chapter).

The Basic Options Quote

Because the pros want to know immediately what options they are buying or selling, they have combined four options characteristics into a single quote. For example:

IBM July 90 Call

Underlying stock: IBM
Type of option: Call
Last day of trading: Third Friday in July
Strike price: $90

Microsoft December 25 Put

Underlying stock: Microsoft
Type of option: Put
Last day of trading: Third Friday in December
Strike price: $25

Tracking, Inc., January 15 Call

Underlying stock: Tracking, Inc.
Type of option: Call
Last day of trading: Third Friday in January
Strike price: $15

The Detailed Options Quote

Before the Internet, it wasn't easy to get access to real-time options quotes. You either had to wait for the next day's newspaper, visit your local brokerage firm, or call up your account representative. Now you can retrieve options quotes instantaneously on several Web sites.

In addition, before the arrival of computers, you had to memorize dozens of letter and number combinations to read an options quote. Now the quotes are so user-friendly that it's easy to find what you need quickly. You might wonder how all this information—the underlying stock, the strike price, the expiration date, and the type of option—can be put into a five-digit code. But a system was cleverly figured out. (Note: It's possible that a new system will be created in the future that will be even less confusing.)

Let's begin by looking at the detailed options quote in Figure 3-1. By the way, the quote is called an *option chain*, because it contains a *series* of options, in this case, for Boeing. Eventually I will analyze with you all of the information on this very important screen. It's essential that you learn how to read an option chain. After all, if you confuse your quotes, you could end up buying or selling the wrong option. For example, it is very common to make money-losing mistakes because you confuse the strike price and expiration dates.

BA   **BOEING CO**

Last	72.69	↓	-1.44	Bid	72.51	Size	1

Calls

Trade	Symbol	Date - Strike	Last	Change	Bid	Ask	Open Int
Trade	-BACN	Mar 18 06 70.00	$3.30	-$1.10	$3.20	$3.30	3501
Trade	-BACV	Mar 18 06 72.50	$1.50	-$1.30	$1.35	$1.45	51
Trade	-BACO	Mar 18 06 75.00	$0.40	-$0.45	$0.40	$0.45	5358
Trade	-BADV	Apr 22 06 72.50	$2.45	-$0.95	$2.40	$2.50	220
Trade	-BADO	Apr 22 06 75.00	$1.30	-$0.55	$1.25	$1.35	437
Trade	-BAEU	May 20 06 67.50	$6.70	-$1.50	$6.60	$6.80	56
Trade	-BAEN	May 20 06 70.00	$4.80	-$1.20	$4.70	$4.90	3539
Trade	-BAEV	May 20 06 72.50	$3.20	-$0.90	$3.10	$3.30	2618
Trade	-BAEO	May 20 06 75.00	$2.05	-$0.65	$1.95	$2.05	5396
Trade	-BAEP	May 20 06 80.00	$0.55	-$0.35	$0.55	$0.65	2307
Trade	-BAHP	Aug 19 06 80.00	$1.90	-$0.40	$1.85	$1.95	2750

BA   **BOEING CO**

Last	72.69	↓	-1.44	Bid	72.51	Size	1

Puts

Trade	Symbol	Date - Strike	Last	Change	Bid	Ask	Open Int
Trade	-BAON	Mar 18 06 70.00	$0.35	$0.15	$0.25	$0.35	2561
Trade	-BAOV	Mar 18 06 72.50	$1.05	$0.45	$1.00	$1.10	303
Trade	-BAOO	Mar 18 06 75.00	$2.64	$1.04	$2.50	$2.65	1709
Trade	-BAPN	Apr 22 06 70.00	$1.00	$0.40	$0.85	$0.95	675
Trade	-BAPV	Apr 22 06 72.50	$1.75	$0.65	$1.75	$1.85	481
Trade	-BAPO	Apr 22 06 75.00	$3.10	$0.90	$3.10	$3.20	380
Trade	-BAQL	May 20 06 60.00	$0.20	$0.05	$0.15	$0.20	1542
Trade	-BAQM	May 20 06 65.00	$0.55	$0.10	$0.50	$0.60	2729
Trade	-BAQN	May 20 06 70.00	$1.55	$0.40	$1.50	$1.60	4113
Trade	-BAQV	May 20 06 72.50	$2.60	$0.70	$2.45	$2.55	2731
Trade	-BATV	Aug 19 06 72.50	$3.80	$0.70	$3.60	$3.80	60
Trade	-BATO	Aug 19 06 75.00	$5.00	$0.80	$4.90	$5.00	2371

Figure 3-1   **Option Chain: Boeing**

Although each brokerage firm might have slightly different ways of displaying an option chain, Figure 3-1 gives you an idea of how an actual quote would appear on your screen. Your brokerage firm has the option chain on its Web site. If you don't have a broker, you can go to a couple of sites that list the option chain. Although dozens of Web sites provide a free option chain, the most well known are the Chicago Board of Options Exchange (CBOE) Web site (www.cboe.com), the Options Industry Council (OIC) Web site (www.888options.com), the MSN financial Web site (www.moneycentral.com), and the options link at Yahoo! Finance (finance.yahoo.com).

To look up an option quote, enter the letters of the stock symbol, such as BA or IBM. On the left, select "options," and the option chain will be displayed. If this doesn't meet your needs, go to a search engine such as Google and type "Option Quote." You should have no problem finding free option quotes.

Unusual Facts about Options Quotes

As I said, you no longer have to memorize option symbols because the brokerage firms display the entire symbol with user-friendly codes. A few points to remember:

1. Many of the companies with two- or three-digit stock symbols have a similar options symbol. Sometimes you'll see unusual two- or three-digit codes. For example, you might see MSF or MSQ for Microsoft, whereas the base option symbol for General Electric (GE) is GE. And some, like Citigroup, use only one letter (C) as their root symbol. *Note*: Nasdaq stocks use only three letters for their root symbol (shortened from four letters).
2. Expiration dates are assigned three option cycles: one beginning in January, one in February, and one in March.
3. Strike prices are usually displayed on the option chain as follows: If the stock price is under $25, the strike prices are in increments of 2.5 points. If the stock price is between $25 and $200 a share, the strike prices are in increments of 5 points. And if the stock price is over $200 a share, the strike prices are in increments of 10 points. On occasion, there are exceptions to these rules.

The Super Secret Options Quote Code Book

You might wonder what the letter and number combinations of an options quote means. Actually, before the Internet became popular, the options exchanges created special symbols that let options traders know all the most important information in an option. The purpose of the codes was to save space. Each option symbol is constructed as follows: Name of Underlying Stock–Expiration Date–Strike Price.

For example, the IBM July 90 Call is actually coded as: IBMGR. How do I know this? Because I can look it up in the code book.

Month	Call Code	Put Code
January	*A*	*M*
February	*B*	*N*
March	*C*	*O*
April	*D*	*P*
May	*E*	*Q*
June	*F*	*R*
July	*G*	*S*
August	*H*	*T*
September	*I*	*U*
October	*J*	*V*
November	*K*	*W*
December	*L*	*X*

Figure 3-2   Call/Put Codes

In Figure 3-2, you see the code for the expiration dates. So using the IBM July 90 Call as an example, we look up July and notice the symbols *G* and *S*. Since this is a call, G is the correct code for the expiration date. So with one letter, you can determine the expiration month and whether it's a call or put.

Next, let's determine the strike price. When you look at the code book in Figure 3-3, you see a list of all the strike prices in five-point increments. Using the IBM July 90 Call as an example, you look up the 90 strike price, which is specified by the letter *R*. Therefore, the option symbol for the IBM July 90 Call is **IBMGR**.

Code	Strike Prices		
A	5	105	205
B	10	110	210
C	15	115	215
D	20	120	220
E	25	125	225
F	30	130	230
G	35	135	235
H	40	140	240
I	45	145	245
J	50	150	250
K	55	155	255
L	60	160	260
M	65	165	265
N	70	170	270
O	75	175	275
P	80	180	280
Q	85	185	285
R	90	190	290
S	95	195	295
T	100	200	300
U	7.5	-	-
V	12.5	-	-
W	17.5	-	-
X	22.5	-	-

Figure 3-3   Strike Prices

For fun, try to do two on your own. I will give you the underlying stock, whether it's a call or put, the expiration month, and strike price, and you tell me the option symbol. Ready?

What is the symbol for the IBM January 65 Call? The answer: IBMAM.

What is the symbol for the IBM March 95 Put? The answer: IBMOS.

Because most brokerage firms write out the symbols for the options contract, it's not essential you memorize the options symbols. Of course, if the symbols are eventually changed, there will be even less reason for you to memorize the codes. Nevertheless, it's a good idea to understand how the symbols are constructed and what they actually mean.

. . . .

Now that you have a general overview of the options market, you're going to learn how to trade. In Part Two you will learn almost everything you need to know about a popular strategy called *selling covered calls*. For some of you, this might be the only options strategy you will ever use.

PART TWO

SELLING COVERED CALLS

4

The Joy of Selling (Writing) Covered Calls

You've waited a long time to apply all of the isolated bits of knowledge we've discussed so you can finally begin trading. Learning the strategies is not that difficult. The difficulty lies in the fact that for each strategy, you have many choices of what to do. In the stock market, you really have three decisions: buy, hold, or sell. But with options, the choices are seemingly endless. (Why do you think they call them options?)

In Part Two we are going to discuss almost all you need to know about *selling* or *writing covered calls*. It's not necessarily easy to learn, especially at first, although it's considered a conservative options strategy. Selling covered calls is mostly used to generate income or cash flow, which is why it's so popular with both professionals and individual investors who use options to manage their stock portfolios.

This is the strategy that my risk-averse friends will appreciate (although there can be some risk, which we will discuss in Chapter 6). If you talk to certain speculators, they might claim that selling covered calls is boring. They prefer other options strategies whereby they can do more leveraging. My answer to them is "When is it boring to make money?" To use a baseball analogy, while you're waiting to hit a home run, why not hit a few singles?

Nevertheless, this will be a challenging chapter. You may even have to read it a couple of times before you truly understand it. To trade options, you have to consider everything carefully, even when using a so-called simple strategy like selling covered calls.

I'll be straight with you: Part Two is perhaps the most important section in the book. Why? Because much of what you wanted to know about options can be taught using covered calls. If you learn and understand this strategy, the other options strategies will seem relatively easy.

What It Means to Sell a Covered Call

Remember when I asked you earlier if you wanted to be a buyer or a seller? When you use the covered call strategy, you will be a seller. That's right—you are going to sell call options to people like my speculator friends. And even if you aren't interested in selling covered calls, it is important to understand how a seller thinks. This information can be useful no matter what side of the options contract you take: buyer or seller.

In options talk, *selling* a call is the same as *writing* a call. In the days before computers, sellers had to write the orders on special forms, so the term *writing a call* stuck with many of the old-timers. In the options market, people use both terms interchangeably, saying that they are writing, or selling, a call. In this book, I will use *selling calls* rather than *writing calls* because it is more precise.

There is something else you should know about selling calls. When you sell a call on a stock that you own, it is known as a *covered call*. The word *covered* means that your position is protected because you own shares of the stock you are selling. Therefore, in this section I talk only about selling options on stocks that you have already bought and own in your brokerage firm's account. The official definition of selling a covered call from the Options Industry Council (OIC) is "An option strategy in which a call option is written against an equivalent amount of long stock." Not too bad.

My explanation will take a little longer. When you sell a covered call, you are selling the buyer the right to buy your stock. To many people, it sounds weird to sell a right. Unlike investing in stocks, you are not holding a stock certificate or a piece of a company. In fact, you never get to hold the options contract that gives you this right. Your only evidence that you bought or sold an option is what appears on your account statement or computer screen.

First of all, keep in mind that to sell a covered call, you must own a stock. So when you sell a covered call, your stock is tied up. Basically, you have handed the rights to sell the stock to the buyer. Now the buyer controls the rights to the stock until the expiration date. If you want to be really technical, you have handed your right to sell the stock to your broker. The call buyer technically has nothing to do with what goes on with your stock.

There is one main reason you are willing to sell covered calls and give up your right to sell the stock. You want to receive compensation, that is, money. Do you remember the name of the money you receive from the buyer? If you do, you're catching on quickly. The compensation you receive from the buyer is called the *premium*. This is the main reason why you want to sell covered calls in the first place.

Many covered call sellers are preoccupied with receiving monthly or quarterly income. The premium is their reward for selling the covered call to someone else. Later, when we go through the steps of selling a covered call, you will be able to calculate exactly how much premium you might receive.

The Advantages of Selling Covered Calls

There are actually two very good reasons to sell covered calls:

1. You can use options to bring in income or increase cash flow.
2. You can use options as a method to sell stock that you own.

When we talk about increasing income or cash flow, it means that you sell covered calls to buyers for the sole purpose of receiving money. Instead of working for your money, your money is working for you. If you are clever, you can figure out ways to bring in relatively consistent income.

But there are other advantages as well. Not only do you receive the premium, but you still own the stock. That means if the stock goes up in price, you receive capital gains. In addition, you also receive dividends from owning stock in the company (if the company has dividends).

In addition, a very clever covered call strategy is to use the options market to sell stock you were thinking of selling anyway. You might as well receive a few extra bucks for doing so. There are thousands of buyers who will gladly give you their money.

Selling covered calls is similar to buying a house and renting it out to someone else. But instead of renting your house, you are renting your stocks. What if you don't own any stock? Don't worry. After you learn this strategy, you can actually look for stocks to buy just so you can sell call options on them. You need to think like a seller—much like the woman who sold an option on the house she owned and the manufacturing company that sold an option on snow shovels.

There are other good reasons for selling covered calls. It's one of the few options strategies that you can use in an IRA or in a tax-deferred account like a 401(k). Selling covered calls is considered a conservative strategy and is allowed by the Securities and Exchange Commission (SEC). Perhaps the best reason for selling calls in an IRA or 401(k) is that you won't be taxed on the revenue you receive (depending on the rules of the pension plan). Be sure to contact a tax advisor to confirm this is correct for your plan.

Perhaps you may be thinking that selling covered calls is too good to be true. Obviously, there are downsides to every strategy, and later in Chapter 6 the risks of selling calls will be thoroughly discussed. That's why I'll take so much time in the next three chapters to explain your various options (no pun intended).

Meanwhile, a lot of what you need to learn about options can be taught with covered calls. So, let's get started. I think you'll enjoy this intriguing strategy.

Background

The current date is February 27. Figure 4-1 illustrates the most active March through August call options for Boeing Company (NYSE: BA). The current price of Boeing is $72.69 a share (although it's guar-

	BA	BOEING CO						
Last	72.69	↓ -1.44		Bid	72.51		Size	1
						Calls		
Trade	Symbol	Date - Strike	Last	Change	Bid	Ask	Open Int
Trade	-BACN	Mar 18 06 70.00	$3.30	-$1.10	$3.20	$3.30	3501
Trade	-BACV	Mar 18 06 72.50	$1.50	-$1.30	$1.35	$1.45	51
Trade	-BACO	Mar 18 06 75.00	$0.40	-$0.45	$0.40	$0.45	5358
Trade	-BADV	Apr 22 06 72.50	$2.45	-$0.95	$2.40	$2.50	220
Trade	-BADO	Apr 22 06 75.00	$1.30	-$0.55	$1.25	$1.35	437
Trade	-BAEU	May 20 06 67.50	$6.70	-$1.50	$6.60	$6.80	56
Trade	-BAEN	May 20 06 70.00	$4.80	-$1.20	$4.70	$4.90	3539
Trade	-BAEV	May 20 06 72.50	$3.20	-$0.90	$3.10	$3.30	2618
Trade	-BAEO	May 20 06 75.00	$2.05	-$0.65	$1.95	$2.05	5396
Trade	-BAEP	May 20 06 80.00	$0.55	-$0.35	$0.55	$0.65	2307
Trade	-BAHP	Aug 19 06 80.00	$1.90	-$0.40	$1.85	$1.95	2750

Figure 4-1   Option Chain: Boeing Calls
Source: Fidelity Investments. Copyright 2002 FMR Corp. All rights reserved.

anteed to change by the time you read this). You already own 100 shares of the stock.

Understanding Covered Calls

We will sign onto our brokerage firm's account and enter the symbol of the underlying stock—in this case, BA. As soon as it is entered, the Boeing option chain suddenly appears on your screen (see Figure 4-1). You can find the option chain on your brokerage firm's site or on Web sites such as the OIC, the MSN Web site, or Yahoo!.

The Premium

The option chain contains a great deal of information. First of all, because we are selling calls, we are focused on the *premium*, which is often displayed as the *bid price*. The bid price simply displays the option buyers' best price. This is also the amount of money you'll receive if you are selling covered calls. Just as in the stock market, the bid price changes constantly, especially on active options.

The premium you receive (bid price) is displayed as per contract cost, from slightly above zero to $6.60 in this example, but premiums range from pennies to hundreds of dollars. You may be wondering why there is such a wide range of premium prices. Welcome to the options market. Understanding premiums is one of the keys to being a profitable options seller.

Remember that the current price for the underlying stock, Boeing, is $72.69. We'll choose the Boeing April 75 strike price (Symbol: BADO) because it's so close to the current price. Later I'll teach you how to select a profitable strike price. When you look at Figure 4-1, you see that the premium is currently displayed as $1.25 per contract.

To calculate how much you'll receive if you sell the call, we'll take out our calculator. Remember that one option contract equals 100 shares of stock.

Turn Calculator On   How Much Premium You'll Receive

$1.25 per contract premium (April 75 call)
× 100 shares of Boeing stock (or one option contract)

Total: $125 premium

Explanation: Because the premium is $1.25 a contract and a contract equals 100 shares of stock, then the premium you will receive for selling this stock will be $125. If you sold 2 contracts, you would receive $250. If you sold 5 contracts, you would receive $625. If you sold 10 contracts, you would receive $1,250. Remember that to sell 10 contracts, or 1,000 shares, you first have to own 1,000 shares of Boeing.

Let's say that you wanted to sell the covered calls for a later month. Take a look at the Boeing May 75 strike price. When you look it up, the premium is a bit higher—$1.95 per contract. Do you know why the premium is higher?

Hint: The later the expiration month, the higher the premium.

Let's take out our calculator.

Turn Calculator On   How Much Premium You'll Receive

$1.95 per contract premium (May 75 calls)
× 100 shares of IBM stock (or one option contract)

Total: $195 premium

Explanation: Because the premium is $1.95 per contract and a contract equals 100 shares of stock, then the premium you would receive for selling this contract is $195. If you sold 2 contracts, you would receive $390. If you sold 5 contracts, you would receive $975. If you sold 10 contracts, you would receive $1,950. Once again, you must own 1,000 shares of Boeing to receive the premium on 10 calls.

The most enjoyable part of selling covered calls is calculating how much premium you're going to get. Just don't make the common mistake of spending the money before you receive it! A few days after you sell the covered call, the cash (premium) you receive goes into your brokerage firm's account marked as Credit Received.

It's All about the Money

A few years ago, I discovered the beauty of covered calls. I sat down with a calculator and computer, looking up the premiums on dozens of options and calculating how much money I was going to make. It seemed like such an easy way to bring in extra cash (and from the comfort of my own home).

I figured I could bring in thousands of dollars in extra income every few months by selling covered calls on stocks I owned. But after jumping into it a bit too quickly, I realized that selling covered calls was a little more involved than I had originally thought. Although I made money every few months, it wasn't easy. Unfortunately, the books available at the time were either too technical or too unrealistic. I am determined to prevent you from making the same mistakes that I did.

That is why it's so important that you learn the following terms. These terms become especially important when you are buying calls and puts. At first, it will seem a little confusing until you have more practice using them.

Introducing At-the-Money, Out-of-the-Money, In-the-Money

The terms *at-the-money*, *out-of-the-money*, and *in-the-money* will help you determine if your options are profitable. By the time you finish

BA		BOEING CO						
Last	72.69	↓	-1.44	Bid	72.51	Size		1
						Calls		
Trade	Symbol	Date - Strike	Last	Change	Bid	Ask	Open Int
Trade	-BACN	Mar 18 06 70.00	$3.30	-$1.10	$3.20	$3.30	3501
Trade	-BACV	Mar 18 06 72.50	$1.50	-$1.30	$1.35	$1.45	51
Trade	-BACO	Mar 18 06 75.00	$0.40	-$0.45	$0.40	$0.45	5358
Trade	-BADV	Apr 22 06 72.50	$2.45	-$0.95	$2.40	$2.50	220
Trade	-BADO	Apr 22 06 75.00	$1.30	-$0.55	$1.25	$1.35	437
Trade	-BAEU	May 20 06 67.50	$6.70	-$1.50	$6.60	$6.80	56
Trade	-BAEN	May 20 06 70.00	$4.80	-$1.20	$4.70	$4.90	3539
Trade	-BAEV	May 20 06 72.50	$3.20	-$0.90	$3.10	$3.30	2618
Trade	-BAEO	May 20 06 75.00	$2.05	-$0.65	$1.95	$2.05	5396
Trade	-BAEP	May 20 06 80.00	$0.55	-$0.35	$0.55	$0.65	2307
Trade	-BAHP	Aug 19 06 80.00	$1.90	-$0.40	$1.85	$1.95	2750

Figure 4-2 Option Chain: Boeing Calls
Source: Fidelity Investments. Copyright 2002 FMR Corp. All rights reserved.

this book, you will be very familiar with these terms. When you actually start trading options, the first thing you want to know is if your option is at-the-money, out-of-the-money, or in-the-money. You may wonder which is best. The answer is that it all depends on the options strategy you are using.

To make it easier to understand these terms, let's bring up the Boeing option chain again. See Figure 4-2.

At-the-Money

Rule: When the current price of the stock is the same as the strike price, the option is said to be at-the-money. People will say it's at-the-money even if it's a few pennies away.

As you can see, the current price of Boeing is $72.69. Now look at the various strike prices, from 70 to 80.

Using the screen shown in Figure 4-2 as an example, the 72.50 strike price is almost at-the-money. This is very important so I'll give another example. If the current price of General Electric (NYSE: GE) is $35 a share, what strike price is at-the-money? If you answered 35, then you are right. It could be the February 35, the March 35, or the April 35, but 35 is at-the-money.

You may be wondering how this helps you. I promise that when we begin discussing covered call strategies, all of this will make sense.

Out-of-the-Money

Rule: When the strike price of the option is higher than the price of the underlying stock, the call option is out-of-the-money.

Using Boeing as an example, the next closest strike price *above* $72.69 is out-of-the-money. (The pros will say the option is one strike price away.) Therefore, the March 75 is out-of-the-money. So is the April 75. The March 75 is approximately two points out-of-the-money. The May 80 is more than seven points out-of-the-money. What about the August 80? That is also out-of-the-money.

> *Advanced Hint*: Notice that the more the option is out-of-the-money, that is, the higher the strike price, the less expensive the premium. For example, the May 80 is only $0.55 while the May 75 is a respectable $1.95.

In-the-Money

Rule: When the strike price of the option is lower than the price of the underlying stock, the call option is in-the-money. In fact, the in-the-money option is the opposite of the out-of-the-money option.

In the example in Figure 4-2, the next closest strike price *below* $72.69 is in-the-money. Therefore, the March 70 is in-the-money. So is the May 70. The May 67.50 is more than five points in-the-money. The March 70 is almost 3 points in-the-money.

> *Advanced Hint*: Notice that the more the option is in-the-money, that is, the lower the strike price, the more expensive the premium. For example, the March 70 is more expensive than the March 72.50.

The chart below should help you understand whether your call option is out-of-the-money, at-the-money, or in-the-money.

Is it Out-of-the-Money, At-the-Money, or In-the-Money?

Assume that the underlying stock is at $30 a share.

Strike Price	Call Option
$40	Far out-of-the-money
$35	Out-of-the-money
$30	At-the-money
$25	In-the-money
$20	Deep in-the-money

Note: Later on in the book, you will learn why you need to know if an option is in-, out-, or at-the-money.

The Art of Exercising Options

Until now, you have been holding all the cards (to use a poker analogy). You get to choose the underlying stock, pick the premium, and decide which expiration date is best for you. When you sell a covered call, it seems as though all you have to do is collect the premium (that's also how some authors make it seem).

You may wonder what the buyer (also called the *call holder* or *holder*) gets out of the deal. The answer is simple but powerful: Remember that when you sell a call you give up your right to decide when the stock is sold, but the buyer can decide to call the stock at any time. Put another way, the buyer has the right, but not the obligation, to purchase the stock. This is a very big deal.

When the call holder buys the stock from you, he or she is *exercising* the option. When the call holder *exercises* the option, you are required to deliver the shares of stock on which you sold calls. Don't worry—it's all done automatically through the computer so you don't actually have to do anything.

From the covered call seller's perspective, which is your perspective, the stock you owned is suddenly taken from your account and sold at the strike price. You also get paid at the strike price. There is actually an official term for what happens to your stock when the buyer exercises the option. The stock is said to be *assigned* or *called away* at the strike price. Because *called away* so clearly describes what happens to your stock, that is the term I'll use.

Once again, at what price does the buyer exercise the option? If you said at the strike price, then you are correct. If the buyer decides to exercise the option, it's always at the strike price. That is according to the rules of the options contract.

In summary, you could wake up one morning and discover that the stock on which you sold calls has been called away at the strike price. In other words, the buyer decided to exercise his or her right to buy the stock. You keep the premium, any past dividends, and any capital gains, but the stock is no longer in your account. You could always buy the stock back and sell calls on it the next month. A lot of people do this every month.

Let's see what happens behind the scenes. When the buyer decides to exercise the option at the strike price, the brokerage firm notifies the Option Clearing Corporation (OCC). After the OCC takes over, it selects, at random, a brokerage firm with a matching option. Then the brokerage firm notifies you, the call seller, that your stock has been assigned or called away. At that moment, your stock will be sold at the strike price. By the way, you have no control over whether the stock is called away. That is completely up to the buyer.

Note: In case I didn't make this clear. Your stock can be called away at any time until expiration (although it's usually done close to the expiration date).

The Unexercised Option

What happens if the stock never makes it to the strike price? This happens a lot more often than you might think. Although there is some controversy over the exact numbers, it has been reported that most options expire unexercised by the expiration date. No one agrees on the exact percentage.

Nevertheless, if the option doesn't gets exercised, you get to "pocket the premium" and keep the stock. You also get to sell another call on the same stock if you wish. Some would say this is the perfect outcome. Perhaps that's why many sellers secretly hope the stock never makes it to the strike price.

When Do Buyers Exercise Their Options?

Do you want to know when a buyer will exercise an option? This is actually a fascinating question, one that is the key to understanding covered calls. The answer is that this will usually happen when the stock price is above the strike price of the options contract and when expiration has arrived.

If at the end of the expiration period, the stock price is above the strike price, even by $0.05, your stock will almost surely be called away. I can almost guarantee it. So if you are going to sell covered calls, you have to expect your stock to be called away at expiration.

Here's another interesting fact. Most of the time, the stock will be called away on the expiration date, that is, the third Friday of the month. That's right—usually the buyer will wait until the last minute to exercise the option (on occasion, the day before). So when you sell a covered call, you must be prepared to wait until the very last day before the stock is called away from you.

Of course, there are exceptions. On rare occasions, a stock will be called away from you before the expiration date. And it's extremely rare, almost unheard of, for someone to exercise an option that is not in-the-money. The reason is they would lose money, and no buyer wants to pay more for a stock than he or she has to. If the strike price is higher than the actual price, it'd be silly to buy the stock at the strike price when they could buy it in the stock market for a better price.

Fascinating Facts about Exercising Options

1. American-style options, the ones discussed in this book, can be exercised at any time on or before the expiration date. European-style options, however, can be exercised *only* on the expiration date.
2. You don't have to do anything to sell your stock. You usually find out the Monday after the third Friday of the month if your stock was called away.
3. It is very easy to get mixed up when talking about exercising an option. Remember, the *option* is exercised by the buyer of the contract. When selling a covered call, after the *option* is exercised, the stock is called away from the call seller.

The Options Market Finally Gets Respect

It took almost a hundred years, but an organized options market was finally created, based on the successful trading platform of the futures market. This is a short account of how the options market finally got the respect it deserved, after a very rough start.

1960s

During most of the twentieth century, trading in the over-the-counter options market was still rather slow and tedious. Because there was no organized options exchange, trades were done by telephone. An options dealer (what we now call a *market maker*) arranged the deal between the buyer and seller. In return, the market maker was paid the difference between the bid and the ask price, known as the *spread*. Unfortunately, because there wasn't an organization to guarantee contracts, traders didn't really know an option's fair price. As a result, the public had little interest in trading options.

The most annoying rule during this time was one mandating that if an options contract needed to be exercised, it had to be done in person. That means that if you missed the option exercise deadline, your option would be voided even if your option was profitable.

In 1968, the Chicago Board of Trade (CBOT) looked at the over-the-counter options market and concluded that changes needed to be made. It realized that at a minimum, options contracts needed to be standardized; that is, the terms of a contract had to be the same for all contracts. In addition, the rule about exercising in person was eliminated.

1970s and Beyond

In 1973, after four years of study and planning, the CBOT applied to the SEC to create the world's first stock options exchange, called the Chicago Board Options Exchange (CBOE). The CBOE and the American Stock Exchange (which had allowed options trading on its floor) created an organization that would issue the contracts and guarantee the "settlement and performance" of the contracts. And thus the Options Clearing Corporation (OCC) was created to issue, settle, and guarantee options contracts.

Officially, the OCC is a corporation owned by five of the six U.S. exchanges that trade listed stock options. In addition, the OCC creates a liquid options market.

With all of the paperwork and politics out of the way, the CBOE opened for business on April 26, 1973. The first options trading room was actually the smoking lounge for CBOT members. According to the authors of *Options* (McGraw-Hill, 1999), critics wondered how a bunch of "grain traders from Chicago thought they could successfully market a new trading instrument that the New York Stock Exchange had judged too complex for the investment public."

Call options were allowed on 16 of the stocks in the most widely known American companies. It would be another four years before put options were introduced. The first day, there was a total volume of 911 options contracts. By the next year, the average daily volume was 6,000 contracts. with an annual volume of 1 million contracts.

By the end of 1974, after banks and insurance companies included options in their portfolios, the average daily volume in the options exchanges zoomed to over 200,000 contracts. Soon, other stock exchanges began trading listed options. Once the daily newspapers began listing options prices, volume multiplied even more.

With the introduction of computers, wireless devices, and additional options products, the average daily volume at the six options exchanges is now 6 million. The annual volume is 1.5 billion contracts. Ironically, the volume of trading in the first half hour often exceeds the volume of options contracts for all of 1974.

. . . .

Now that you have been introduced to the covered call strategy, you will learn how to choose profitable covered calls.

C H A P T E R

How to Choose Profitable Covered Calls

By now, you might be feeling rather comfortable with the idea of selling covered calls. Maybe you think the art of picking the right call is simply looking up the most expensive premium and selling calls on it. Unfortunately, this is what many people do, but it's not necessarily the best method. The pros call it *chasing premiums*. Some people think the hardest part is deciding how much money they want to make!

What you may not realize is that there is an art to picking the right covered call, and premium is only one part of the equation. In this chapter, we'll look closely at all of the factors that lead us to a profitable covered call.

Until now, most of our time was spent looking at definitions. In this chapter, however, we are going to do a lot more thinking and analyzing. That is what makes options so challenging. Selling covered calls, like other options strategies, is similar to playing a game of chess. You'll see why as we look at the main factors that affect the covered call. As a matter of fact, these factors affect all options.

Market environment
Underlying stock
Strike price
Premium
Expiration date
Interest rates*
Dividends*

Advanced note: Interest rates and dividends will be discussed in Chapter 10.

When you understand how each of these factors affects the covered call, then you will be on your way to becoming a successful covered call trader.

The Ideal Market Environment for Covered Calls

If you trade stocks or invest in the stock market, you want the market to go up—and not just by a little—by a lot. In fact, the more volatile the stock market, the better for you, especially if the market is going higher. The one market environment that most people hate is a flat, trendless market that appears to go in circles. In this type of market, stocks seem listless and out of breath, and no one seems to be making any money. The stock market could put you to sleep.

But there is one group of people who welcome a sideways, do-nothing market. Do you know who? If you guessed the seller of covered calls, you are right. The ideal market environment for selling calls is when the market appears to be going nowhere. In this type of market, there is little danger that the market, or your underlying stock, will fall. Obviously, there are no guarantees, but your trade could be more successful when the market is lifeless. While everyone is complaining they can't make any money in the stock market, you are cleaning up.

Question: If the covered call seller prefers a flat market, then you are right to assume he or she likes stocks that act the same way. Do you know why the covered call seller wants a flat market and stocks that aren't going anywhere? If you're not sure of the answer, you will be by the end of the chapter.

Searching for the Ideal Underlying Stock

At this point, you either already own stocks or are thinking of buying a stock that you want to sell calls on. You already know that the underlying stock is important, but many people underestimate *how* important. In fact, one of the keys to finding a profitable covered call is finding a profitable underlying stock.

Actually, the underlying stock is essential no matter what option strategy you use. Most people mistakenly have it reversed. They first look at the option, then at the stock. They are led to believe that the winning options are out there waiting to be discovered, like a winning lottery ticket. Unfortunately, they are looking in the wrong place. The right place, of course, is at the underlying stock.

So what are the specific characteristics you are looking for in the underlying stock? You are looking for a well-known company that is fairly liquid (meaning a lot of people are trading it) and that is slowly and steadily moving upward. It isn't very volatile and stays within a tight and predictable range. Not too high, not too low, but just right. If you can find stocks like these, you might consider buying them for the sole purpose of selling covered calls.

For many years, investors and institutions sold covered calls on stocks of companies like General Electric, Coca Cola, IBM, and Home Depot. These stocks fit the covered call profile. Many of the stocks in the Dow Jones Industrial Average (DJIA) were also perfect for this strategy. Although these stocks worked out well in the past, unfortunately there is no guarantee they will work in the future.

To find the ideal underlying stock, you have to do research. And once you find this ideal stock, you can sell covered calls on it month after month, quarter after quarter. Perhaps you already own one of these ideal stocks. If so, it will save you the trouble of looking for another one.

How do you find these ideal stocks? You have to start by using the tools of the stock market, that is, fundamental and technical analysis. By combining both technical and fundamental analysis, you should find the criteria for dozens of companies that you would like to own. In addition, most brokerage firms have stock screeners that will help you find specific attributes.

Perhaps you're still not sure why it's so important when using this strategy to have a flat or slightly bullish market environment and stocks that are slowly moving up. To help convince you, let's first take a look at the kinds of stocks you don't want to use with a covered call strategy.

The Wrong Underlying Stock

The kinds of stocks on which you want to avoid selling covered calls are the ones that go up or down and are too volatile. In other words, they move too quickly in one direction or the other. For example, roller-coaster technology stocks like Google would be too risky to sell calls on. Just because Google doesn't fit our criteria for a profitable covered call prospect has nothing to do with the worth of the company.

So what is the problem with a very liquid stock like Google? Actually, the high-volume, high-volatile stocks like Google have extremely high premiums. People will pay dearly to own options in a company like Google. But as a covered call seller, you can't be tempted by the high premiums that this volatile stock brings.

As a seller of covered calls, you don't want stocks that make huge moves in one direction or another—the kind of stocks that surprise you on Monday morning. Although volatile stocks have rich premiums, for a covered call seller these kinds of stocks should be avoided. The reason is that the downside risk is too great.

For example, if you sell calls on a wild stock like Google (at least it was wild in the past), the stock could drop by dozens of points—and you can't sell it.

Advanced Note: In Chapter 7, I will show you a way to buy back your option in case of an emergency.

Therefore, the biggest risk to selling covered calls is that the underlying stock falls too much and although you keep the premium, you lose money as the stock drops. So you want to stay away from stocks that are going down in value, perhaps even breaking through moving averages and showing other technical weaknesses.

On the other hand, if an underlying stock like Google moves up too quickly, you will still make money but you will miss out on any gains past the strike price.

Hint: Keep in mind that the option premium is not the determining factor in an option trade. There are other factors such as the strike price, the underlying stock price, and how much time is left to expiration. Basically, when you are deciding whether an option is a good buy or not, the premium must be considered, but look at other option characteristics. This will make more sense as you gain more trading experience.

The Characteristics of a Profitable Covered Call

You already know that to find a profitable covered call, you have to search for the ideal underlying stock. Let's assume you use technical and fundamental analysis to find one of those stocks. Next, you have to dig a little deeper and look at specific factors, including the most profitable premium, the correct strike price, and where the stock will be on the expiration date. All of these factors must be weighed and studied before you can make the right decision, a decision that will bring you the most profits without risking your capital or tying up your stock for very long.

Thinking Your Way to Profits

I'll pull up the Boeing option chain again (see Figure 5-1) to help analyze all of the characteristics you'll need to search for a profitable covered call.

The Strike Price

There are many factors to consider when choosing a strike price. At first, you might think of choosing the strike price with the most expen-

BA		BOEING CO					
Last	72.69	↓	-1.44	Bid	72.51	Size	1

					Calls		
Trade	Symbol	Date - Strike	Last	Change	Bid	Ask	Open Int
Trade	-BACN	Mar 18 06 70.00	$3.30	-$1.10	$3.20	$3.30	3501
Trade	-BACV	Mar 18 06 72.50	$1.50	-$1.30	$1.35	$1.45	51
Trade	-BACO	Mar 18 06 75.00	$0.40	-$0.45	$0.40	$0.45	5358
Trade	-BADV	Apr 22 06 72.50	$2.45	-$0.95	$2.40	$2.50	220
Trade	-BADO	Apr 22 06 75.00	$1.30	-$0.55	$1.25	$1.35	437
Trade	-BAEU	May 20 06 67.50	$6.70	-$1.50	$6.60	$6.80	56
Trade	-BAEN	May 20 06 70.00	$4.80	-$1.20	$4.70	$4.90	3539
Trade	-BAEV	May 20 06 72.50	$3.20	-$0.90	$3.10	$3.30	2618
Trade	-BAEO	May 20 06 75.00	$2.05	-$0.65	$1.95	$2.05	5396
Trade	-BAEP	May 20 06 80.00	$0.55	-$0.35	$0.55	$0.65	2307
Trade	-BAHP	Aug 19 06 80.00	$1.90	-$0.40	$1.85	$1.95	2750

Figure 5-1   Option Chain: Boeing Calls
Source: Fidelity Investments. Copyright 2002 FMR Corp. All rights reserved.

sive premium. This is not necessarily the best choice, and you'll soon see why.

Once again, Boeing is at $72.69. If you want to sell a covered call on this stock, you have many strike price choices. You have to decide in advance what strike price is ideal for what you are trying to accomplish.

If you select an option that is out-of-the-money or far out-of-the-money, then you know that you have some room on the upside before it's called away (if it's ever called away). Therefore, the advantage of selecting out-of-the-money calls is that you know there is less chance that the stock will be called away from you.

On the other hand, the higher the strike price and the farther the option is out-of-the-money, the less premium you'll receive. For example, when we look at the Boeing option chain in Figure 5-1, we see that the out-of-the-money Boeing May 80 premium is a paltry $0.55. It's not even worth your time to sell this contract, as the premium for one call will bring in only $55.

The Boeing May 85 option (not shown on the screen) fares even worse. This is also out-of-the-money but because it has an 85 strike price, the premium is worth only $0.10. The chances that the stock will hit the strike price are remote, and the premium reflects those odds.

Let's see what happens if you select an option that is only slightly out-of-the-money, for example, the Boeing April 75 call option. The premium on the April 75 call is $1.25. If Boeing actually makes it to $75 a share (or higher) at expiration, the stock will probably be called away. Even if Boeing goes as high as $78 or $80 a share, the stock will be sold at $75 a share. As mentioned earlier, there is a very good chance that the buyer will exercise the option on the expiration day, the third Friday in April.

But what if Boeing doesn't go up but goes down? First, the value of the options contract goes down also. If the stock continues to lose value, it is offset by the value of the contract that you sold.

For example, if you sold the April 75 contract for $1.25 and Boeing goes down to $68.00, the value of the contract might drop to $.75. You could buy it back for a $.50 gain.

If Boeing continues to drop, the value of the covered call contract will drop. Once again, you could buy the contract back (this strategy is discussed in Chapter 7). The reason you might consider buying back the option is to lessen the potential loss. Fortunately, the covered call helps to offset the loss in the underlying stock.

So which strike price is best? The best strike price is the one the investor is most comfortable with. The comfort range is determined by the expiration date, premium, and volatility (discussed in Chapter 10). The strike price also depends on your outlook for the stock, the outlook for the market, and how much risk you want to take.

As you can see, choosing a profitable covered call is more involved than many people realize. Many people underestimate how much thinking is involved when using this strategy. Therefore, choosing a strike price is an important decision that you shouldn't take lightly.

Advanced Note: You shouldn't make a blanket statement whether it's best to sell in-, at-, or out-of-the-money calls. It's easy to make a case for each strategy, depending on whether you are bullish or bearish towards the underlying stock. For example, some traders like at-the-money strike prices. If the stock stays in a narrow range, then the at-the-money strike price might be desirable. Others prefer the in-the-money strike price because it provides protection and profit potential. On the other hand, the stock will likely be called away if it's still in-the-money at expiration. And finally, the out-of-the-money strike price gives you less premium but more upside potential. In addition, if the option is out-of-the-money at expiration, the stock will not be called away. As you can see, you have many choices depending on your strategy.

Premium

Although premium should not be the only factor in determining which options to sell, it is definitely an important factor. After all, this is your payment. So premium must always be considered when looking at options characteristics. You are in the business of selling covered calls to make as much money as possible with the least amount of risk.

Therefore, you want a premium that is paying at least $0.50 or more, although $0.75 or $1.00 is even better. The reason for this is simple. Let's say you sell a call on a premium worth $0.50. If you are selling only one call, all you'll receive is $50 in premium. After you subtract the $10 to $15 in commissions, you almost broke even. You'd have to write 10 contracts to bring in decent income.

If you are going to sell only one covered call, you'll want premiums that are at least a dollar. Anything less than that is really not worth your effort. If you are selling five calls or more, you can grab $0.50 premiums although $0.75 would be better. Most covered call sellers aim for between $1 and $3 in premium. This will bring in between $100 and $300 for one call, $500 and $1,500 for five calls, and $1,000 to $3,000 for 10 calls.

Note: Keep in mind that you also want to avoid grabbing juicy premiums on falling stocks—not a recommended strategy.

Expiration Date

There is an old Rolling Stones song titled *Time Is on My Side*. When you sell covered calls, time *is* on your side. It's not important to you if the clock is ticking. If the stock doesn't reach the strike price before the expiration date, the option expires and is worthless. You keep the premium *and* the stock—the nearly perfect ending to a successful trade.

When you look at the Boeing option chain in Figure 5-1, you'll notice the March 75 is worth $0.40, the April 75 is worth $1.25, and the May 75 is worth $1.95. If you went three months out, the premium would be even higher. Therefore, you can conclude that the farther out the expiration date, the higher the premium. And the farther out the month, the longer your stock (and your money) is tied up. On the other hand, the closer you get to the expiration date, the less the option is worth. All of these factors have to be considered when you are searching for a profitable covered call.

So what is the ideal expiration date? Once again, it depends on your strategy. Many investors believe that a minimum of one month is best, while three months is even better. The longer the expiration date, the more premium you'll receive. And yet, you also must be willing to let your stock be tied up for that long. On the other hand, a 2-week covered call can be risky while providing good reward potential. As usual, you have to experiment with different expiration dates to see which ones work best for you.

Here's how a professional trader friend of mine put it all together: "At $0.25, it's not worth it to me. The lowest I would go is $0.50 with two weeks left to expiration. With a month left, I would go for a dollar. The most I would ever do is three months. And if you are out for three months, you're looking for a premium of at least $2.00 to $3.00."

Conclusion: What Is a Profitable Covered Call?

After talking to professional traders as well as relying on my personal experience and extensive research, the profile of a potentially profitable covered call is clear (although there are no guarantees). And the winner is...

· ·

A profitable covered call = a relatively high premium with a strike price and expiration date that gives you the highest reward with the least risk.

· ·

You could choose an out-of-the-money call that is one strike price away from the stock price. If you chose two strike prices away, the premium may not be desirable. Regarding the expiration date, a minimum

of one month is ideal. Although a longer expiration date brings a higher premium, perhaps you don't want your stock tied up for that long. And finally, aim for at least $0.75 in premium, but more if possible.
You will eventually find a profitable covered call by observing and thinking. It takes study and research to find these stocks. There are software programs that will give you ideas (but no magic answers). It's really up to you to find stocks (and options) that fit the criteria you are looking for.

Caveat: If you are a professional trader, it would be easy to find fault with what is considered a profitable covered call. After all, there are a number of expert strategies that contradict these conditions. But you have to start somewhere, and if you are a novice trader, start with the criteria listed above.

As you gain more experience, you can tweak your criteria, perhaps lengthening the expiration date or choosing a near-the-money strike price. Most importantly, as soon as you can devise your own criteria for defining the ideal strike price, you will be on your way to becoming a successful options trader. Your ultimate goal is independence. Then you don't have to depend on authors or instructors or other traders to tell you which options to trade and what strategy to use.
Before you put this book down and fire up your computer, remember this. There is a big difference between knowing what a profitable covered call is and finding it. Unfortunately, what you see on paper often has nothing to do with how a stock trades in the real world.

The Futures Market

Although the options market was created based on the successful platform of the futures market, they are completely different markets. This is an account of how the futures market was created and what happens behind the scenes.

History
The futures market can be traced back to Japan during the Middle Ages where commodities like silk and rice were traded in advance of a certain date (although informal trading of futures contracts

were recorded in England as early as the 13th century). In Chicago, however, the futures market was created to help farmers sell their grain in advance of the harvest so they could receive money to help survive the rest of the year.

As a result, in 1848, Midwestern grain traders, along with wealthy Chicago businessmen, created the Chicago Board of Trade (CBOT). They wanted a central location for the buying and selling of agricultural contracts.

In 1865, the Chicago Board of Trade created standardized contracts, called *futures contracts* (or *forward contracts*), for buying grain from Chicago area farmers. Trading of grain and other agricultural products was conducted on the trading floor of the exchange, affectionately called *the pit*. This is the place where members screamed and shouted at each other, called *open outcry*, using hand gestures to signal the price and quantity of contracts. Each commodity had its own designated pit.

In 1919, the Chicago Butter and Egg Board, an offshoot of the Chicago Board of Trade, changed its name to the Chicago Mercantile Exchange (CME, or "the Merc"). Even today, the CBOT and the Merc are the two largest futures exchanges in the world.

The terminology of the futures market is quite similar to the options market. For example, a futures contract is called a *derivative*, which means it is derived from an underlying asset such as corn, soybean, or currency. In fact, the options market is an extension of the futures market and the stock market, based on the successful model created by those exchanges.

In the futures market, people buy and sell commodities like agricultural items (sugar, corn, coffee), currencies (dollar, euro), precious metals (gold, silver), petroleum products (heating oil, gasoline), interest rate products (Treasuries, Fed Fund rates), and stock indexes (Nikkei, Dax, Dow).

The futures market is huge, exceeding the number of trades in the New York Stock Exchange. For example, the equity markets are measured in billions of dollars but the futures markets are measured in trillions.

When you enter into an agreement in the futures market, you agree to take delivery of the actual commodities. (Imagine what the neighbors will think if 3,000 bushels of corn are dropped on your front lawn.) In recent years, although open outcry is still used, the futures exchanges also allow electronic trading using wireless devices. For example, you could trade currencies from your home using a laptop computer. The two types of traders who primarily use the futures market are speculators and hedgers. Hedgers use the futures market as an insurance policy, to protect their product or lock in a price. For example, a company like Starbucks will use the futures market to lock in the price of coffee and will obviously take delivery of the product.

Speculators, on the other hand, use the futures market to increase income and make profits, just as they do in the equity markets. They have no desire to take physical delivery of the commodity but just want to make money. Therefore, unless you really want to take delivery of 3,000 bushels of corn, you can simply buy and sell the contracts.

The futures market uses a form of margining called *mark to market*. If a futures contract is worth $1,000 and the contract drops by $500 by the end of the day, $500 is taken out of your account. In addition to mark-to-market rules, futures trades are also *cash-secured*, meaning your account must be paid off or settled in cash by the end of the day.

Behind the Scenes at the Futures Market

To get a feel for what goes on in the futures market, I talked to a former independent options and futures trader, Howard Korn-stein, who trades securities from his home. He said the futures market can get pretty wild at times. "Trading commodities is one of the most speculative transactions you can make in the financial markets," he says. "If you are a novice and want to speculate in futures, you will be in for a big surprise." Undisciplined speculators will likely lose most of their money, he claims, probably within a week.

He said the futures market is not a place for beginners because you can lose more money than you started with. "Not only can you lose more than you put in, but you are required to pay up at the end of the day or they'll close the contract down." Many amateur futures traders are surprised by these nightly margin calls.

"If the contract is worth $1,000," Kornstein says, "by the end of the day you could theoretically lose $4,000 or $5,000. Even if you have a stop loss, if there is breaking news, the contract can blow through your stop and go limit down."

Kornstein says that an appropriate use of the futures market is if you are a large company. "In 2005, several airlines hedged their accounts by buying futures contracts for jet fuel," Kornstein explained. "At the time the contracts were selling for $0.80 to $0.90."

According to Kornstein, the cost of fuel tripled, so the airlines that hedged against the rising price of fuel made out pretty well. The contracts zoomed to $1.50, the closing strike price of jet fuel at the time. "Three airlines took delivery of the fuel, and instead of paying $1.50, they paid only $0.80," he said. The airlines that didn't hedge paid triple for fuel that summer. The companies that hedged showed a profit for the year whereas most other airlines booked a loss.

Kornstein says that another way to use the futures market is as a hedge against the rise in prices. Hedgers, however, are willing to take possession of the product while speculators are not.

The bottom line is that the futures market, although a useful and necessary trading platform, is not recommended for casual traders. At a minimum, you should master the options market before even thinking about speculating in futures.

• •

Now that you've learned the factors you need to choose profitable covered calls, you'll learn the mechanics of selling covered calls.

6

Step-by-Step: Selling Covered Calls

In this chapter, we are going through the actual steps of selling covered calls. Believe it or not, this is the easiest part of selling a call. The brokerage firms have spent millions of dollars to make the buying and selling of options as simple as possible—some might even say fun.

You've already signed the options agreement with your brokerage firm. I assume you have spent the time studying dozens of underlying stocks until you find one that meets the criteria we discussed. Perhaps you already own a stock that you want to sell calls on.

Before we get started, however, let's discuss some of the risks of selling covered calls. Don't worry—I'm not trying to talk you out of trading. Although selling covered calls is considered one of the safest options strategies, you should understand all the risks thoroughly before you place your first trade. Unfortunately, no options strategy is completely fail-safe, including selling covered calls.

Any professional trader will tell you that one of the most important actions you can take before placing a trade is planning for the worst-case scenario. If you enter a trade with visions of profits dancing in your head but no clear idea of the potential risks, you could lose money. So please pay close attention to all of the things that could go wrong when using this strategy.

The Risks of Selling Covered Calls

There are risks in selling covered calls just as there are risks in everything related to the financial markets. If you want to avoid risk completely, then put your money in a certificate of deposit (CD) or a Treasury bill. Because you are reading this book, I assume you are willing to accept some risk. Therefore, read what could go wrong and plan accordingly. Although you can never eliminate risk completely, you can learn to manage it.

Heart-Stopping Plunges

The biggest risk of selling covered calls is that your underlying stock drops in value—a big-time drop—like those in Enron and a whole slew of Internet stocks in the late nineties (we're talking about 80 to 90 percent drops). If you had sold calls on Enron, you wouldn't think this is such a great strategy. If you sell calls on volatile stocks, don't forget the buyer is in control. All you can do is watch helplessly as the stock falls.

Advanced Note: In case of emergency, there is an option strategy that allows you to buy back your option and take back control of the stock (introduced in Chapter 7).

Nevertheless, it is important to find stable stocks, the kind that won't make you lose sleep. As long as the contract remains valid, no matter what the price of the underlying stock, you are at the mercy of the buyer. Otherwise, you have to wait until the expiration date before the stock is either sold or left in your account. Although you still keep the premium, which will reduce the pain a little, you could lose money from the underlying stock if it suddenly drops.

Lost Opportunity

The other problem with selling calls is what's called the *risk of lost opportunity*, or the potential loss of future profits. For example, let's say you sell a call on Boeing at the strike price of $75, and it suddenly zooms up from $72.69 a share to $80 or higher. You get to keep your premium and you get whatever you gained on the stock, but anything higher than your strike price is not yours. The stock will almost surely be called away at $75 a share no matter how high Boeing goes. This can be very frustrating to people who don't want to be left out when a stock makes a sudden move upward. Some people don't like covered calls because you have purposely limited your future gains. You will not make more than the strike price, but the premium received will help to reduce the loss of the position if the stock reverses.

Margin

Although you can't borrow from the brokerage to sell options (this is called *trading on margin*), you can buy the underlying stock on margin and then write calls against it. One of my trader friends had this to say about using margin to buy the underlying stock: "Because you are borrowing money, if market conditions change, you are risking a greater amount of money than you have. You could be overextending yourself."

If the underlying stock goes down in price while you are on margin, then your losses will accumulate very quickly, and you could get the dreaded margin call. Believe me, the premium from selling the covered call won't completely save you. If you are using margin to sell covered calls, you are taking on too much risk. Generally, it's not recommended to borrow money to buy stocks.

Stop Losses

Because you have given up the right to control when the underlying stock is sold, then you have given up your right to enter a stop loss order on the stock. That means if you are going to use a stop loss, you should enter it prior to starting a covered call position.

Advanced Note: Technically, you are allowed to use a stop loss on a covered call, but it involves a number of advanced steps. Sometimes the broker won't allow it, so check with the brokerage firm first. A better strategy is a collar (described in Chapter 14) that protects the underlying stock in case of unexpected price drops.

Unrealistic Expectations

Although it's possible to routinely profit by selling covered calls on a monthly or quarterly basis, there are no guarantees. Although receiving regular income from selling covered calls is a worthy goal, it can take time to find profitable premiums. Once again, if you sell covered calls, you must be prepared to have your stock called away at anytime. On the other hand, some people use covered calls as a method to sell stocks they no longer want. They purposely want their stocks called away. This strategy will be explained in Chapter 7.

How to Reduce Risk

Many people, even after hearing the risks, want to go out and sell calls on all their stocks or buy stocks just to sell more calls on them. Please wait. Before you plunge into the covered call strategy, think about the following suggestions to reduce risk.

Get Organized

One of the best ways to reduce risk is to become organized. In fact, if you don't keep track of your trades, then you will never know if you are profitable or not. You need to write down the strike price, the expiration date, how much premium you received, and other important information. If you are going to sell covered calls on a regular basis, you must be organized. One way of getting organized is to keep a trading diary for entering all important information.

Start a Trading Diary

It seems that all the top traders have a journal or diary where they enter their trades. After all, how do you know you've succeeded unless you know how you got there? The covered call seller enters all the essential information, including the names of underlying stocks to watch. Some traders call it their *stalk list*. If you are going to sell covered calls, you must keep close track of all essential information, as well as write down what went wrong or right. If you don't write it down, you won't learn from your mistakes.

Know the Importance of Discipline

Everyone talks about the importance of discipline but few know what it means. In your trading diary, you should include a set of rules that will guide you when buying or selling options. It's not enough to have rules. You must also have enough courage and faith in your judgment to follow your rules.

Start by Paper Trading

Another idea is to "paper trade," or use the brokerage firm's software to practice. Unfortunately, because you are not using real money, paper trading often doesn't truly simulate the emotional roller coaster of real trading. Because it's only simulated trading, you won't experience the gut-wrenching pain of losing real money. Nevertheless, paper trading helps you to learn the different options strategies.

Start Small

When you are first starting out, begin by selling only one call, representing 100 shares. By starting small, you'll keep your losses and emotions under control, while tweaking your strategies and techniques. Don't make the mistake of jumping into the options market with too much money and too little knowledge.

What to Expect from the Covered Call Strategy

Figure 6-1 gives a visual representation of the risks and rewards of selling covered calls. It shows both the advantages and disadvantages of the covered call strategy. One of the major criticisms of the strategy is that potential losses are substantial if the stock plummets, whereas profits are limited.

On the other hand, you can't have it both ways. If you are looking for slow and steady returns, then the covered call strategy might meet

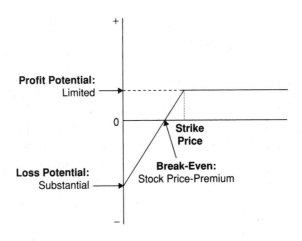

Figure 6-1   Risks and Rewards of Selling Covered Calls
Source: CBOE. Copyright 2006 All rights reserved.

your needs. If you are searching for huge profits, then you'll want to read Chapter 8. Only you can decide if the covered call strategy makes sense for you and what you are trying to achieve.

Now that we've discussed the risks of using this strategy, it's time to learn how to trade. If you don't have a brokerage account (and even if you do), refer to the figures below to show you step-by-step how to sell covered calls.

If at first you are uncomfortable placing your own orders or want help from the brokerage firm, the representatives would be happy to assist you. They can do several things for you, such as steer you to the correct strike price or expiration date, and confirm that the covered call order you placed makes sense. Reputable brokerage firms want you to make good transactions and don't want you to lose money.

In the option chain, you have already looked up the option symbol, strike price, and expiration date. In fact, before you place the order, you should know well in advance exactly what covered call you are selling.

Let's Begin Trading!

In this example, you have 100 shares of Boeing in your brokerage account and now you want to sell one covered call. As you gain more experience, you can sell calls on as many shares as you have in your account. We'll pull up the Boeing option chain in Figure 6-2 to confirm the strike price, expiration date, and premium.

1. The current quote on Boeing is $72.69.
2. In Figure 6-2, the option symbol we are interested in selling is BADO.
3. You have chosen the April 75 call (the expiration date is seven weeks away), an option that is out-of-the-money.
4. The bid on the April 75 call is $1.25. This is the premium you will receive.

Figure 6-3 shows a sample options entry screen for covered calls. The screens on your brokerage account might look different than those displayed here. And remember, by the time you read this book, the options displayed here will have expired. This is true for every option chain in this book.

BA		BOEING CO					
Last	**72.69**	↓	-1.44	Bid	**72.51**	Size	1

					Calls		
Trade	Symbol	Date - Strike	Last	Change	Bid	Ask	Open Int
Trade	-BACN	Mar 18 06 70.00	$3.30	-$1.10	$3.20	$3.30	3501
Trade	-BACV	Mar 18 06 72.50	$1.50	-$1.30	$1.35	$1.45	51
Trade	-BACO	Mar 18 06 75.00	$0.40	-$0.45	$0.40	$0.45	5358
Trade	-BADV	Apr 22 06 72.50	$2.45	-$0.95	$2.40	$2.50	220
Trade	-BADO	Apr 22 06 75.00	$1.30	-$0.55	$1.25	$1.35	437
Trade	-BAEU	May 20 06 67.50	$6.70	-$1.50	$6.60	$6.80	56
Trade	-BAEN	May 20 06 70.00	$4.80	-$1.20	$4.70	$4.90	3539
Trade	-BAEV	May 20 06 72.50	$3.20	-$0.90	$3.10	$3.30	2618
Trade	-BAEO	May 20 06 75.00	$2.05	-$0.65	$1.95	$2.05	5396
Trade	-BAEP	May 20 06 80.00	$0.55	-$0.35	$0.55	$0.65	2307
Trade	-BAHP	Aug 19 06 80.00	$1.90	-$0.40	$1.85	$1.95	2750

Figure 6-2   Option Chain: Boeing Calls
Source: Fidelity Investments. Copyright 2002 FMR Corp. All rights reserved.

Account	Symbol	Last	Chg.	Bid	Ask	Action	Qty	Order Type	Price
	-BADO	1.30	-0.55	1.25	1.35				

□ Skip Order Preview   Add Another Order

Figure 6-3   Covered Call Order Entry
Source: Fidelity Investments. Copyright 2002 FMR Corp. All rights reserved.

Account Name or Number

If you have more than one account, be sure the correct account is entered. One mistake that many people make is making trades from the wrong account.

ACTION: *You enter the account number or name.*

Symbol

Be sure the correct option symbol appears on the screen. It doesn't hurt to double-check. Because you are trading options, some brokerage firms require you to enter a special symbol like a dash before the quote.

Warning: If you enter the option for an underlying stock that you don't own, you are suddenly switching from selling a covered call to selling an uncovered, or naked, call. If you thought selling calls was risky before, you should see what happens now. More than likely, the brokerage firm's software will prevent you from proceeding; nevertheless, you want to be careful.

Bottom line: Always make sure you are entering the correct option symbol.

ACTION: *You enter the option symbol for the underlying stock you own in your account.*

Last, Change, Bid, and Ask Price

The option's last sale price, how much it changed, and the current bid and ask price are automatically displayed for you. Because you are selling covered calls, you will focus primarily on the premium that you will receive from the buyer. Usually, it will be at or near the bid price.

> *Hint*: The last price is rather deceptive. It could be five minutes ago, five hours, or even five days ago.

Sell to Open

In Figure 6-4, you need to select the correct options transaction. This is important.

As you should know by now, options have their own unique language. When you are ready to enter an order, you need to memorize or post what is meant by the following terms. It's essential you fully understand what they mean. You have four choices.

> *Buy to Open*: Select this when buying calls or puts. It's used to initiate or create a long position.
>
> *Sell to Close*: Select this when you are closing out or selling a call or put that you have previously bought.
>
> *Sell to Open:* Select this when you are selling calls or puts, including selling covered calls. (Most often used to initiate a covered call position.)
>
> *Buy to Close*: Select this when you are closing out or decreasing a call or put position that you have previously sold. You also select this when you want to close a covered call position prior to expiration.

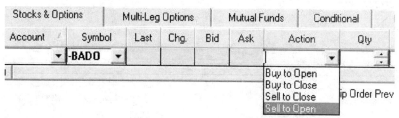

Figure 6-4 Sell to Open Order Entry
Source: Fidelity Investments. Copyright 2002 FMR Corp. All rights reserved.

Because you are selling covered calls, we will select **Sell to Open,** because in options terminology you have just opened or created a new position to sell a covered call.

ACTION: *You enter Sell to Open.*

Quantity

Because you are selling one contract (or 100 shares of the underlying stock), you enter the number "1." Remember that one of the most common mistakes is entering the number of shares rather than the number of contracts. This is a mistake made by many people, even the pros on occasion (perhaps only the careless ones). Be sure you don't mix shares and contracts. If you do make a mistake and enter 100, the system will hopefully prevent you from going any further.

ACTION: *You enter 1 contract for 100 shares. More than likely, you'll never enter more than 10 contracts, or 1,000 shares.*

Order Type: Market or Limit Order

In Figure 6-5, you need to choose between a market order or limit order.

If you are familiar with the stock market, you know that you can choose to let the market fill your order (*market order*) or you can choose your own price (*limit order*). It's generally agreed that choosing a limit order is better. Then you decide the price at which you will buy or sell. You can let your brokerage firm "work" the order to try and get a better price.

Symbol	Last	Chg.	Bid	Ask	Action	Qty	Order Type	Price
-BADO ▼	1.40	0.00	0.00	0.00	Sell to Open ▼	1 ▲▼	▼	▲▼
							Market	
							Limit	
				□ Skip Order Pre	Stop Loss	ther Order

Figure 6-5   Market or Limit Order Entry Screen
Source: Fidelity Investments. Copyright 2002 FMR Corp. All rights reserved.

As an options trader, the more control you have over your order, the better, so it's suggested you place a limit order. Keep in mind that just because you select a limit order doesn't mean you will be filled at the price you selected.

ACTION: *You select limit order.*

Price

Using the Boeing option BADO as an example, the bid price is $1.25 (it might change by the time you're ready to place the order). Although you can try and get a better price, perhaps by adding a few pennies, it's unlikely. If you are ready to place your covered call order now, just enter the current bid price and your order could be filled immediately.

If you are selling covered calls, it's not worth your time to pinch pennies. One old trick is to enter the ask price, which is higher than the bid price. You can enter it but it's unlikely you will get filled, at least not right away.

ACTION: *Enter the current bid price of $1.25. You'll receive $125 in premium, which is placed in your account.*

Time Limit

You have a choice of when you want the order filled. You can choose Day or Good 'til Canceled. See Figure 6-6. Because you are selling a covered call and thus want the order filled as soon as possible, you will select Day, meaning that you want the order filled by the end of the day or the order will be canceled. More than likely, the order will be filled immediately (if you're selling at the bid price, that is).

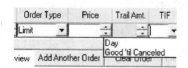

Figure 6-6   Select Time Limit

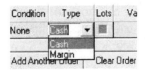

Figure 6-7   Select Cash or Margin

Type of Account

If you have both an IRA and a regular brokerage account, you might have to choose between a cash or margin account. See Figure 6-7. For example, if you have only a 401(k) or IRA, you can sell covered calls, but it's probably a cash account. And if you have only a brokerage account, it's probably designated as a margin account.

ACTION: *Select cash or margin (only if you have multiple accounts).*

Preview Your Order

If there is a preview button, it's always recommended that you review your order before you press the enter key. In the preview screen, the commission and the total cost of the order are usually displayed. You'd be amazed at the number of mistakes people make when entering an order, and the preview button allows you one more chance to make corrections.

Broker Instructions: If you called your broker and wanted to place the above order by phone, you would say, "I want to sell one covered call for Boeing April 75 at a limit price of $1.25 (or better) good for the day only."

Note: If you do decide to place a call with a broker, the recorded telephone call is a valid contract. Be sure to speak clearly and use options terminology to place the trade.

Press the Enter Key

As soon as you press the enter key, the order will be routed to an options exchange. A buyer will be matched to your sell order. In a few days, the premium will be placed into your account as credit received. Congratulations. You have sold your first covered call. Before you relax, however, you need to closely monitor your option position. This might not be the best time to take a vacation.

Employee Stock Options

If you are one of the 10 million employees who received stock options, then learning more about your rights could save you a lot of aggravation. Most publicly traded corporations offer stock options, often as a reward or to let employees share in the success of the company. They are usually delivered on a quarterly or yearly basis. Most important, the options given to employees are not the same as those for sale in the options market (the kind discussed in this book).

When a company "grants" stock options to an employee, it gives the person the right, but not the obligation, to buy a certain number of shares in the company at the current market value. Unlike options traded on an exchange, however, employee stock options are issued by the company and are sometimes not transferable. In addition, employees can't sell or trade the stock options to a third party. More than likely, there will be other restrictions.

For example, the employee won't be able to exercise the options until a certain date in the future, perhaps in one or two years, maybe longer. Eventually, the employee can exercise the options and convert them to stock. The stock can then be sold on the open market. You should know that these accounts are monitored closely by the company's human resources department. Individuals who sell these stock options before the restricted date could find themselves out of a job or passed up for future promotions.

Since many stock options are issued without a dollar value, they might not be considered as taxable income. In addition, when the options are exercised, after being held for at least a year, it will likely be at the more favorable long-term capital gains tax rate.

Nevertheless, it's essential that you consult a tax attorney or advisor to confirm the specific rules of your stock option plan. If you receive stock options, it is *your* responsibility to speak to the managers of the stock option program, as well as to a tax advisor.

Find out the tax ramifications, when you should exercise, the limitations, and restrictions of the plan. Employees of companies that offer stock option programs should closely examine the restrictions of both the stock and options distribution. You want to avoid any surprises.

For example, one of the reasons the employees of Enron were so angry was they were restricted from buying or selling stocks and options in their 401(k) plan. On the other hand, the executive officers of the company were not restricted. Although the officers of Enron sold their stocks and options when the stock went down, Enron employees were left with nearly worthless stocks and options.

During the late 1990s, many Enron employees decided to hold their options contracts rather than exercise. Although these employees paid capital gains tax on the current value of the options, by the time they sold the options, they were nearly worthless. Others exercised their stock options and dutifully held their stocks so they could get the lower long-term capital gains tax rates. When the stock plunged, however, the Enron employees ended up owing tax on income that had disappeared.

There have been other horror stories. For example, with some employee stock plans, options are a taxable event on the day they are issued, so employees have to pay a short-term capital gains tax. In cases like this, the individual didn't exercise the option and kept it as an open contract. By the time they're ready to exercise, the stock is worth much less. Basically, the individual paid tax on stocks that have little or no value.

If you are an employee receiving stock options from your employer, once again, it's *essential* that you find out everything you can about your rights and obligations. Consult with a tax attorney or tax advisor so you don't get snagged by a tax event that seemingly comes out of nowhere.

. . . .

Now that you've learned the mechanics of selling covered calls, you'll learn how to manage and maintain your covered call position.

Managing Your Covered Call Position

Now that you have received the premium for your first covered call, you might think that all you have to do is sit back and wait until the expiration date. This would be a serious mistake, one that many people make. After you press the enter key and submit the order, the real work begins.

After all, stocks are as unpredictable as people (maybe more so), and when you are putting your money on the line, anything can happen. That is why it's so important to plan for any possible scenario. Therefore, one of the most useful steps you can take is to create a trading plan, which helps you to determine what to do after you sell your first covered call.

The Importance of a Trading Plan

The purpose of a trading plan is to help you prepare in advance for any possible market condition including when to enter or exit a position. You want to think of all the worst-case scenarios and plan accordingly. As you know, one of the trickiest parts of trading options is that you have so many choices. A written trading plan will help you figure out how to prepare for any what-if scenarios. A trading plan also helps you to control your emotions, one of the characteristics of successful traders. Without a trading plan, you are basically trading blind. Many pros review their trading plan each morning before the market opens.

Your Trading Plan

After you press the enter key, there are three possible outcomes for selling covered calls. Although you are technically not in control of the stock until the expiration date, you must closely monitor both the underlying stock as well as the option. In particular, after you sell the call, keep your eye on the underlying stock. No matter what the underlying stock does—rise, fall, or stay the same—it affects what you will do next. To help get you started, let's take a look at a sample trading plan.

To refresh your memory, you sold covered calls on the Boeing April 75 option, BADO, which was $72.69 a share. Earlier, you had entered a bid price of $1.25.

The Underlying Stock Moves Up

Outcome: The stock price moves above the strike price.

What to expect: You should anticipate the stock will be called away by the expiration date. *Hint*: The longer and higher the stock price is above the strike price, the more likely the stock will be called away. Even if the underlying stock is above the strike price by as little as $0.25, the stock will probably be called away.

Analysis: Most of the time, buyers won't exercise the option unless they have squeezed the most profit out of it, which means they'll probably wait until the expiration date to exercise the option. If the stock is above the strike price by the expiration date, even by a few pennies, the stock will likely get called away.

For example, if Boeing moves past the 75 strike price to $75.50, a buyer will exercise the option, and the stock will be called away at the strike price of $75. You, as the stock owner, will be required to deliver the 100 shares of stock to the buyer and get paid at the strike price. Although you have made money by receiving the premium, you won't receive any profits on your stock above $75 a share (even if Boeing moves well above $75 a share). All you can do is wait until the stock is called away on the expiration date.

Nevertheless, you benefit in three ways if the underlying stock is above the strike price.

1. You receive capital gains from the time you bought the stock until it's sold at the 75 strike price.
2. You collect dividends from owning the stock.
3. You keep the premium.

This is why you want to sell calls on stocks that could potentially go higher than the strike price. If you think the price of the stock will go up even higher, sell a higher strike price.

Note: Keep in mind that if you are using the covered call strategy, you have to plan for and expect the stock to be called away. If you can't bear to have your stock sold, for either emotional or tax reasons, then you shouldn't be selling calls on it.

The Underlying Stock Stays the Same

Outcome: The stock price stays at or near the strike price.

What to expect: You should anticipate the stock will not be called away if the stock price and the strike price are the same. Remember: Even if the stock is above the strike price by as little as $0.25, the stock will almost surely be called away.

Analysis: This is actually what many covered call writers consider the ideal scenario. If the underlying stock never makes it to the strike price, you get to keep the premium, and at the end of the expiration period you can sell another call. This is the way to receive the maximum profit from using this strategy.

When you hear people say they repeatedly sell calls, this is
what they mean.

For example, if Boeing stays at or near $75 a share, that's actually
a perfect scenario. The stock probably won't get called away, and you
can sell another covered call for the following month.

Here's how a professional trader friend of mine summarized this
strategy: "There are times when you can buy a stock and continue to
write covered calls and not risk having the stock taken out of your
account. GE used to be like this. IBM used to be like this, as was
Microsoft. They were very popular stocks. Institutions often bought
large blocks of these stocks knowing they would only move one or
two points in a period, and they would write the covered call for that
quarter. They would assume the stock would never make it there. If it
did, fine, they would have it taken out of their account. But more often
than not the stock didn't get called away."

Some people dream of selling covered calls, month after month,
on the same stocks. However, before you start counting your money,
remember that you can't always count on the fact that stocks will stay
within a narrow range for years.

The Underlying Stock Moves Down

Outcome: The stock drops below the strike price.

What to expect: The stock will remain in your account until the
expiration date. *Hint*: You have to monitor the underlying
stock closely for severe declines.

Analysis: If the stock stays below the strike price, you keep the
premium and can write another call for the next month.
Secret wish: Many call sellers secretly hope that the option
is worthless when it expires, that time runs out, and that
the strike price is never reached. Then they can sell another
option for the stock.

As mentioned earlier, however, the major risk of selling calls is that
the underlying stock price unexpectedly drops. For example, if Boeing
drops well below the current price of $72.69 a share, you will lose money
on the falling stock price even though you keep the premium. Although

the pain of a sudden drop is somewhat buffered by the premium, you still don't want to be trapped in a losing position. This is why it's essential to monitor all your option positions closely.

If you believe the underlying stock will bounce back, then you don't have to take action. However, once the stock falls below the "loss point," you might have to consider emergency actions to get out of your option position. Don't panic. One of the worst mistakes you can make is to close out your covered call position at a loss only to watch the stock rebound.

If you are going to sell covered calls, you do need to plan in case the stock goes down. You can do this by calculating the loss point. If the stock price drops below the loss point, you're losing money.

Calculating the Loss Point

There is a calculation you can do to determine when you have to take emergency action. Let's take out our calculator again.

Turn Calculator On   Calculating the Loss Point

$72.69 Boeing stock price
– $1.25 Premium
$71.44 Loss Point

Explanation: Take the credit you received from the covered call—for example, $1.25—and subtract it from the price of the underlying stock, $72.69. The loss point is $71.44. If the stock drops below this price, you are losing more on the underlying stock than the amount you are receiving in premium.

How to Buy Back Your Call Option

Normally, when you sell covered calls, you don't have to do anything except wait until the expiration date. As you know, however, the main disadvantage of selling covered calls is that the underlying stock might fall.

If this happens, you have two choices. You could watch the stock drop and hope it recovers, maybe even reverse direction. Your second choice is to buy back the calls you sold, allowing you to take back control of the stock. You will use this strategy if you believe a falling stock has little hope of reversing and you want to quickly unwind your option position.

This is not a strategy you will use often, but you should be aware of how it works. Keep in mind that you could lose money on the option if you buy it back as well as lose points in the falling stock. Sometimes it's better to take a deep breath and wait until the stock stabilizes. Use technical analysis to determine if the stock is really in danger or if this is just a temporary pullback.

To buy back an option after you sold calls on it, after entering the option symbol on your brokerage order entry screen, select Buy to Close. You are actually buying the contract back so you can close it down. You enter in the current ask price, which is lower than when you bought it (reflecting the lower stock price).

After you buy back your option, you are free from the terms of the options contract and you are now back in control of your stock. You are free to sell your stock at any price you wish.

Advanced Covered Call Strategies

The Buy-Back Strategy

In the previous example, we discussed how to buy back your option in an emergency. What you might not realize is that many covered call traders purposely use a strategy whereby they buy back options.

For example, let's say you sell a covered call for a dollar, which is put into your account as a credit. When you look at the option chain, you see that the premium is now worth only $0.25 with only a couple of weeks left until expiration. Obviously, the combination of time erosion and a falling stock has reduced the premium. So you buy back the option for $0.25, allowing you to pocket a $0.75 profit (your $1.00 premium received minus $0.25 cost to buy the option back = $0.75 profit).

Now that the stock is under your control again, you are free to sell another call for the next month. Normally, you do nothing until expiration. But with this strategy, you buy back the option (select Buy to Close on your brokerage order entry screen) and resell the calls when the premium becomes attractive again. This strategy works best when the stock has temporarily pulled back and could rebound. In theory, you could repeatedly resell the call on the same stock as it gets closer to the expiration date.

Rolling Options Up, Over, or Out

When you roll options up, over, or out, it means you are closing out the covered call contract you are currently holding and opening an identical position with a different strike price or later expiration date. People roll options for various reasons.

Roll Up

Traders will roll up options when they don't want the stock to be called away. When you roll up an option, it means you close out the current position and roll it up to a higher strike price. Your new option position has the same expiration date but a higher strike price. That way, your stock remains in your account, and you gave yourself a little breathing room.

For example, let's say you sold 10 calls of Home Depot with a February 42.50 strike price. When it hits $42 a share, you're sure the stock will be called away from you (because it keeps going higher). So you close out the position by buying it back at the current ask price (once again, select Buy to Close on your brokerage order entry screen). Then you sell another 10 calls on the February 45 strike price. This gives the stock more room to move higher, and you're in no immediate danger of getting called away.

Roll Over or Roll Out

A roll over is also known as a roll forward or roll out. For example, let's say you are still holding the 10 Home Depot February 45 calls. It is unlikely that the stock will reach $45 a share. In this case, you want to keep selling calls on the same stock. So you roll the option over to the March 45. (Basically, you close the February contract, then open a March contract.) Notice that the strike price remains the same; only the expiration date changes.

If you find the right underlying stock, you could make a nice living from rolling options over and over again, month after month. In the old days when brokers made the trade for you, you'd notify them to roll the option over to the next expiration date. Now you can roll options over from your home computer.

The Buy-Write Strategy

Although this is listed under the advanced strategies, a buy-write is actually quite simple. It works like this. When you simultaneously buy a stock and sell a covered call, it's called a buy-write. Nearly all brokerage firms allow you to simultaneously buy the stock and sell the call, and most have a convenient drop-down menu you can select.

A variation of the buy-write strategy is to look for stocks just so you can sell calls on them. Ideally, you will search for underlying stocks that will provide you with a reasonable premium in a reasonable amount of time.

For example, one of my trader friends bought Tyco (NY: TYC) just so he could sell the covered call. He bought 1,000 shares of Tyco at $26.70 and simultaneously wrote (or sold) 10 of the $27.50 calls. The premium was $0.50 with one week left until expiration (not a bad premium with a week left to expiration).

Tyco made it to $27.50 before the expiration date, just as he expected, when it was taken out of his account. The profits were very favorable. He first made $500 from the premium he received by selling the calls ($0.50 times 10 calls, or 1,000 shares = $500). He also made an $800 profit from the stock (it went from $26.70 to $27.50 for a profit of $0.80, or $0.80 times 1,000 shares = $800.) So in one week he made a total of $1,300. If you are going to use this strategy, look for options that are going to expire but still have some premium left.

Using the Options Market to Sell Your Stock

After you hear about this covered call strategy, you may never want to sell your stock in the traditional way again. A very clever use of the options market is to use it to sell stocks that you own and make a few extra bucks in the meantime. Instead of going through a brokerage firm, you are actually selling stocks through the options market.

For example, let's say you own 100 shares of Home Depot at $40 a share. You had been thinking of selling the stock for some time. So instead of selling the stock immediately, you look up the premium and sell the 42.50 strike price (it's one strike price away). You choose a one-month expiration, which is about as long as you want to wait.

If everything goes as planned, you will receive at least a dollar in premium, and assuming the stock moves up two points, it would be called away at the strike price of $42.50. In other words, you are using the options market to sell your stock at $42.50.

The good news is that you receive a little extra income from the sale. This works best if you were thinking of selling the stock anyway. If you are going to use this strategy, then you want to sell the calls as close to the expiration date as possible.

In the worst-case scenario, although you receive and keep the premium, the stock might fall in price (which is always the risk with covered calls). But this might have happened anyway.

The only time this strategy wouldn't be wise is if you need to sell the stock immediately, for example, if the stock is in danger of collapsing.

Half and Half

If you are not sure how many covered calls to sell on your stock, you can sell calls on only half the position. For example, if you own 1,000 shares of Home Depot, you could sell five calls. You have to experiment to see if splitting positions works for you. The only problem with splitting positions is you have to keep very detailed records and it could get confusing.

An Introduction to LEAPS®

Long-Term Equity AnticiPation Securities (LEAPS) are long-term options contracts that allow investors to establish positions that can be maintained for up to three years. The development and introduction of LEAPS by Chicago Board Options Exchange (CBOE) in 1990 added a whole new range of options possibilities, many suited for so-called conservative stock investors.

Most important, LEAPS are nearly identical to traditional options except for the longer time period. Because the options exchanges didn't want LEAPS to get mixed up with standard options, they changed the symbols. Actually, the most interesting fact is that when LEAPS come within a year of expiration, they are no longer classified as LEAPS but change their symbol to that of the standard option.

There are a number of advantages to LEAPS. First, for a lot less money you can buy options on stocks that you might not be able to afford. You'll get some of the benefits of stock ownership without actually owning the stock (but you can't vote or collect regular dividends).

With index LEAPS, you can trade the entire market for extended time periods. Because many LEAPS expire in two years and eight months (although you can exercise equity options before the expiration date), you have more time to develop long-term strategies. Many investors use options as a hedge against either long or short stock positions. In particular, the LEAPS put would allow you a hedge against a long-term stock position.

There are also disadvantages to buying LEAPS. First, buying calls (and puts) is still a speculative strategy, so you'll need to perform more extensive research. In addition, the spreads on LEAPS are a bit wider than with traditional options. This could be a problem if you need to immediately exit the position. In this case, the loss could be greater than you anticipated.

Another disadvantage is that unlike owning stock, LEAPS eventually expire. Therefore, it is not advisable to buy LEAPS when you really want to buy stock. Some people buy

LEAPS instead of stock, and sell covered calls against them. Not recommended.

Perhaps the biggest negative for buying LEAPS is the cost: the options contracts are rather expensive, perhaps half the price of the stock if you purchase an in-the-money LEAPS call. As we mention throughout this book, time is money. So the more time left on the contract, the more money it will cost.

The question you have to ask yourself is: Do you need the extra time? If so, it may justify spending the extra money on a financial instrument that expires in three years. On the other hand, many people decide to buy the underlying stock rather than take a chance on buying LEAPS. Nevertheless, that's a decision only you can make for yourself.

· ·

Now that you've been introduced to the covered call strategy, you're going to learn how to buy calls, which is often used by option traders to speculate. Whether you are interested in speculating or not, it's essential that you understand this strategy.

You might want to take a break before moving to Part Three. After all, there's a big difference between being a seller of options and being a buyer of options. Instead of receiving premium, you will be paying premium to the seller.

PART THREE

HOW TO BUY CALLS

C H A P T E R

8

Introduction to Call Strategies

If you are reading this book because you want to leverage your money to make a lot of money, this is the chapter you've been waiting for. *Buying calls* (you can also say you are *long calls*) is the preferred strategy of speculators, and there is a good reason why. For a fraction of what it costs to buy stocks, you can leverage your money to double, triple, or quadruple your initial investment. If this is what attracted you to the options market, then you are in the right place.

At first glance, buying options seems a lot less complicated than selling them. As you'll see later, the mechanics of buying calls is a breeze. The hard part, as usual, is making a profit. As mentioned earlier, it is estimated that most call options expire unexercised, although no one agrees on the exact percentage.

Many traders agree that it can be tough to make a consistent living as a call buyer (I'll discuss some of the risks in Chapter 11). On the other hand, if you occasionally speculate by buying call options, it is possible to overcome the odds and make money. Quite a few people have done well buying calls, making more money in a week than some do in a year.

As you'll see when you read this chapter, finding a profitable call option takes skill, knowledge, and a deep understanding of how options are priced. Professional options traders take their trading very seriously. But if you don't have the discipline and use options trading as a way of making easy money, you will likely be disappointed.

So take the time to read this section thoroughly. You never know when you might need to use this strategy and buy call options.

What It Means to Buy a Call

The official definition of buying calls, from the Options Industry Council (OIC) is "An option contract that gives the owner the right to buy the underlying security at a specified price (its strike price) for a certain, fixed period of time (until its expiration)." That sums it up quite well.

My explanation is similar. When you buy a call, you have the right to *buy* the underlying stock on or before the expiration date. You are not required to buy the stock, but you can if you wish. Once again, the buyer is sometimes referred to as the *holder*.

In other words, you have the right, but are not required, to buy the underlying stock at the price listed in the options contract. Just like the option you bought on the house or the option you bought on snow shovels (see Chapter 1), you are temporarily acting as the potential owner of the underlying stock. You have the right to buy the underlying stock but are under no obligation to do so.

For the right to potentially own this stock, you have to pay money (the *premium*) to the seller for the privilege of controlling that stock. And in return for this payment, you control the stock and hope to participate in its rising value. Don't forget. When you buy call options, you control the stock.

Why People Buy Calls

Buying calls is an option strategy primarily used by speculators to increase income. When you buy a call, it means you are bullish on the stock market, the index, or the underlying stock. This strategy works best when a particular stock or index makes an explosive move upward in a relatively short period of time. Like most options strategies, you can leverage a relatively small amount of money into a large amount of money, assuming your trade is successful.

You have only one goal: to make as much money as you can in the shortest amount of time. You hope and believe that the underlying stock is going to go up in price. If it does, you could make money, sometimes a lot of money. If it doesn't, then the most you could lose is what you paid for the option.

Call options, like other options, are linked to an underlying stock. If the underlying stock goes up in price, so does the option. When you buy a call option, you are basically long the underlying stock. You hope the underlying stock, and your option, go up in price before the expiration date.

There are a number of plays that you can make with call options.

1. First, you can buy the call with a plan to eventually buy the underlying stock (as you know, this is called exercising your option).
2. Otherwise, after buying the call, you can eventually sell the option for a profit. In fact, most of the people who buy calls have no interest in buying the stock. They are interested in selling the more valuable call option in the open market. The idea is to sell the call contract for a price higher than you paid for it.
3. Finally, if the stock play doesn't work out, you can allow the option to expire worthless or sell for a partial loss.

The Advantages of Buying Calls

Even if you don't think you'll ever buy calls, it is essential that you learn how. As mentioned earlier, all options strategies are based on buying or selling calls and puts. So no matter what options strategies you eventually use, it's likely that you'll need to know how to buy calls.

Low Cost

Perhaps the most attractive part of buying calls is its low cost. For instance, a stock might be selling for $25 a share but the call contract is only one dollar. You basically get to participate in the movement of the stock for a limited time without having to purchase it. Think about it. You go along for the ride but only pay a portion of the cost.

When compared to buying stocks, buying options seems like a bargain. For example, let's say your neighbor tells you about a "once-in-a-lifetime" stock that is going to take off in the next two weeks. Although you know you should never buy stocks based on tips, you are tempted to sink thousands of dollars into the stock. (You imagine how envious you'd be if your neighbor was right and you didn't take advantage of this opportunity.)

Basically, you don't want to risk too much money but you still want to participate. So instead of tying up thousands of dollars in a stock purchase, you buy a call option. More than likely, the neighbor's stock will go nowhere. But instead of potentially losing thousands of dollars, you might only lose a few hundred. (Of course, there is always the remote chance that your neighbor was right.)

Another advantage is that buying calls allows you to buy stocks that are too expensive. For example, let's say you wanted to buy Google when it was over $300 a share (the last time I looked). It was well beyond the financial means of many people. Even 100 shares would cost more than $30,000. But for a fraction of the cost, you could have bought call options on Google and still participated in the stock on its march upward.

How many people knew that Google was going to zoom because of its popular search engine but did nothing about it? And how many people knew that Apple was going to go up because of the Apple i-Pod? And what about the Internet stocks back in the 1990s? All of those stocks would have been ideal option plays (and good investments). Some people do both: buy stock in the company and supplement it with call options.

And finally, buying calls is the strategy of choice if you don't have a lot of money or you don't want to tie up your capital. You need thousands of dollars to get started in the stock market, but only a few hundred to buy call options.

Leverage

The number one reason that speculators are attracted to buying calls can be summed up in one word: *leverage*. For a fraction of the cost, you are able to control many times more than you invested. For example, for only $500 you can potentially "control" $10,000 or more in stock. Many call buyers are willing to take the chance, knowing that they can make many times over their investment through leverage.

Less Risk

I'm sure you've heard how risky options are, but the truth is that many options strategies can be less risky than stocks if used properly. First of all, unlike investing in the stock market, you know in advance how much you can lose. Therefore, you have controlled your risk. When you buy a stock, it's possible you could lose money, a lot of money, but you're not sure how much (unless it goes to zero). When you buy calls, however, although you could still lose money, you won't lose more than you paid for the option.

The advantages of buying calls were clear a few years ago when Enron dropped by over 80 percent in a week. If you had bought the stock, the losses were catastrophic. Had you bought 100 shares of Enron, for example, it might have cost you approximately $10,000. After Enron blew up, you could have lost approximately $9,500 or more. Had you been holding the call option on Enron, the most you would have lost was perhaps $500, the total cost of the call options.

Diversification

A final reason to buy call options is for diversification. Let's say you'd like to buy more shares of IBM, but you already own too many shares of the stock (what the pros call being *overweight*). Buying options can be an inexpensive method of adding to your position without affecting your diversification formulas.

The Right and Wrong Underlying Stocks

When you sold covered calls, you wanted a rather tame market and stocks that were going nowhere. Not so with buying calls. The ideal environment for buying calls is a bull market. The higher and stronger the market goes up, the better it is for call buyers.

During the bull market of the late 1990s, call buyers did very well as a lot of Internet and technology stocks zoomed higher than many people thought possible. As you probably guessed, call buyers look for stocks that have potential to explode on the upside within a short period of time. You want stocks that are active and have a lot of upward action.

The worst market for call buyers is a flat or falling market. Nevertheless, even if the market goes down, your underlying stock could do well, although it takes skill to find stocks that are not following the market trend.

You might wonder where you can find these ideal stocks. As with covered calls, you should use technical or fundamental analysis to find stocks that are either breaking through the resistance level or are leaders in their sector. Underlying stocks that have broken above the 50-day moving average are often good candidates for going long. You can also be on the lookout for stocks by listening to news reports.

Exercising an Option as a Call Buyer

When you sold covered calls, if the call buyer exercised the option, the stock was called away from you. Now that you have traded places and are the call buyer, you are the one who gets to do the exercising. This is a very powerful right.

Once again, the call buyer (which is now you) has the right to exercise the option. When the buyer exercises the option, he or she buys the underlying stock. The power to exercise an option is one of the advantages to being a call buyer. Do you remember at what price the buyer exercises the option? The answer is at the strike price. If you didn't remember, we'll be discussing this later in the chapter.

There are several reasons why you, as the call buyer, would want to exercise the option and buy the underlying stock. First, you might really want to buy the stock. When you exercise the option, you not only have the right to buy the underlying stock but you also might get it at a discount from the current market price.

Note: Many people buy calls for speculation and have no intention of exercising the option. Other people buy calls because they are truly interested in the underlying stock, and plan to exercise the option so they can buy the underlying stock.

What It Means to Exercise Your Option

When you exercise a call option, it simply means you are exchanging your profitable call option and converting it into shares of stock. As you know from our definitions, you are not obligated to exercise, but you have the right to do so. One reason you would exercise a call option is that you believe the stock will keep moving up. By exercising, you can continue to profit if the stock price moves higher.

Caveat: This depends on your strategy and whether you are a trader or investor.

Most buyers wait until the expiration date to exercise their option, but American-style options can technically be exercised at anytime. Once the option is exercised, however, the exercise is irrevocable.

Note: In Chapter 12, I will discuss in detail the mechanics of exercising an option.

What Is Open Interest?

When you look at the option chain in Figure 8-1, you will see a column for Open Int, a useful indicator that is updated once a day. *Open interest* shows a list of open options contracts that are available to be exercised (or expire) and haven't been closed out yet.

Here's how open interest is calculated. If you bought five Boeing calls as an opening position from a seller who was also opening a position, five call contracts would be added to open interest. And if you sold the five calls that you bought to some-

	BA	BOEING CO						
Last	72.69	↓	-1.44	Bid		72.51	Size	1
						Calls		
Trade	Symbol	Date - Strike	Last	Change	Bid	Ask	Open Int
Trade	-BACN	Mar 18 06 70.00	$3.30	-$1.10	$3.20	$3.30	3501
Trade	-BACV	Mar 18 06 72.50	$1.50	-$1.30	$1.35	$1.45	51

Figure 8-1   Open Interest
Source: Fidelity Investments. Copyright 2002 FMR Corp. All rights reserved.

one who was also closing their positions, open interest would be reduced by five calls.

Just as with any marketplace, supply and demand will dictate prices. Therefore, open interest gives you some very important clues as to which options contracts are the most popular—now or at some time in the future.

For example, let's say there are 10,000 call contracts for the February 30 strike price, 5,000 call contracts for the February 35 strike price, and 10 call contracts for the February 40 strike price. What is the market telling us? It's telling us there may not have been an attractive enough price in the February 40 strike to attract buyers or sellers. It also gives a clue that the stock might not get above the 40 strike price. Perhaps the stock will land somewhere between the February 30 and February 35 strike price (although there are no guarantees this will happen).

In Figure 8-1, the March 70 has 3,501 open interest call contracts while the March 72.50 has only 51. You can assume there isn't a lot of interest in the March 72.50 strike price. On the other hand, the March 70 strike price has attracted more attention, and, therefore, is more liquid. When you have a liquid option, the bid-ask spread could also be tighter.

You can also compare the open interest from one day to the next, looking for unusual spikes in activity. If one day there are 10,000 open interest contracts and the next day there are 14,000 contracts, it's obvious some investors believe the underlying stock is going one way or the other.

Another observation: Let's say there are 10,000 open interest call contracts at the 30 strike price, and there are 9,000 open interest put contracts at the 30 strike price, you could deduct that the bears and bulls are split down the middle.

But if there are 10,000 open interest *call* contracts at the 30 strike price and 1,000 open interest *put* contracts at the 30 strike price, you might take an educated guess that ten times more open interest volume is leaning toward the more bullish call position.

Note: Since some of the brokerage firms don't keep records of daily open interest, you'll have to add it in your trading notebook.

Note: Next to the Open Interest column is Volume. This column is not shown in Figure 8-1. Volume indicates how many contracts were traded that day. When you are trading stocks, volume is an extremely important indicator. When trading options, however, open interest is much more useful.

• •

Now that you've been introduced to the buying call strategy, you'll learn what factors you need to look for to choose profitable calls.

How to Choose Profitable Calls

There are many factors that will determine a profitable call option. The key to success is not getting distracted from your goals: price and profit. In other words, you want to get the most competitive price with the highest possible profits. Nevertheless, there are some important concepts introduced in this chapter that you should learn. By the end of this chapter, however, you'll have a much better idea of the attributes to look for when choosing profitable call options.

How Much Will It Cost?

The first question most people ask is how much do options cost? Perhaps they should really be asking how much are they worth. When you were a call seller, you wanted to receive the most premium you could. But as a call buyer, you are looking for a good deal. At first, you might think that you should simply buy the cheapest option you can find. You'll learn that isn't always the wisest choice.

Before we go any further, let's take a look at your ultimate goal and determine if you made a profit. Do you remember these terms from the last section: out-of-the-money, at-the-money, in-the-money? This is so important that we'll do a quick review.

The table below should help you remember whether your call option is in-the-money, out-of-the-money, or at-the-money.

Assume that the underlying stock is at $80 a share.

Strike Price	Call Option
$90	Far out-of-the-money
$85	Out-of-the-money
$80	At-the-money
$75	In-the-money
$70	Deep in-the-money

Now that you have a better understanding of these important terms, let's sign onto our brokerage account and enter the symbol of the underlying stock, Boeing. The option chain for Boeing is shown in Figure 9-1. The current price of Boeing is $72.69 a share.

For now, we're going to select the March 70 calls, which are in-the-money by more than two points. They are trading for $3.30 per contract, which is the ask price. Perhaps you noticed that when we sold covered calls, we selected an out-of-the-money call. Now that you are buying calls, we selected an in-the-money call. By the end of this chapter, you'll understand why.

Let's take out our calculator to determine how much it will cost to buy one contract.

Turn Calculator On   The Cost of an Option

$3.30 per contract (March 70 call)
× 100 shares of Boeing stock

Total: $330

Explanation: To buy 1 March 70 call, it will cost you a total of $330. To buy 2 March 70 calls, it will cost you $660. Five calls will cost you $1,650. Ten calls will cost you $3,300. Although buying 10 calls at this price seems expensive, if you bought the stock, it would cost you approximately $73,000.

	BA		**BOEING CO**				
Last	**72.69**	↓	-1.44	Bid	**72.51**	Size	1

						Calls	
Trade	Symbol	Date - Strike	Last	Change	Bid	Ask	Open Int
Trade	-BACN	Mar 18 06 70.00	$3.30	-$1.10	$3.20	$3.30	3501
Trade	-BACV	Mar 18 06 72.50	$1.50	-$1.30	$1.35	$1.45	51
Trade	-BACO	Mar 18 06 75.00	$0.40	-$0.45	$0.40	$0.45	5358
Trade	-BADN	Apr 22 06 70.00	$4.00	-$0.70	$4.00	$4.20	55
Trade	-BADV	Apr 22 06 72.50	$2.45	-$0.95	$2.40	$2.50	220
Trade	-BADO	Apr 22 06 75.00	$1.30	-$0.55	$1.25	$1.35	437
Trade	-BADP	Apr 22 06 80.00	$0.30	-$0.10	$0.20	$0.30	1282
Trade	-BAEL	May 20 06 60.00	$13.80	-$1.20	$13.30	$13.50	827
Trade	-BAEM	May 20 06 65.00	$8.80	-$1.40	$8.70	$8.90	2209
Trade	-BAEU	May 20 06 67.50	$6.70	-$1.50	$6.60	$6.80	56
Trade	-BAEN	May 20 06 70.00	$4.80	-$1.20	$4.70	$4.90	3539

Figure 9-1   Option Chain: Boeing Calls
Source: Fidelity Investments. Copyright 2002 FMR Corp. All rights reserved.

How Do You Calculate Breakeven?

After you calculate how much the option costs, you want to do a breakeven calculation to determine at what point the option is profitable. Often, when you buy options, you think you are making more money than you really are. But because of a number of factors, especially time erosion, you end up making less than anticipated. Nevertheless, the breakeven calculation will help you determine if your option is profitable.

The formula for calculating breakeven is as follows:

The call strike price + the premium paid = breakeven

Let's turn on our calculator to take an even closer look at breakeven.

Turn Calculator On   Breakeven

$70 strike price
+ 3.30 cost of the option

Total: $73.30 breakeven

Explanation: In this example, the underlying stock, Boeing, has to reach $73.30 a share for you to break even. Anything above $73.30 is profit. If the stock rises high enough over the strike price, the option could follow the exact movement of the underlying stock. Basically, they will trade in unison. As you probably guessed, by the time the underlying stock has reached this point, the stock is well above the strike price (and deep in-the-money, as the pros like to say).

Advanced Note: Before exercising an option, be sure you calculate breakeven or you could lose money. Many traders exercise the option without calculating the true cost, resulting in a loss.

Now that we finished our review, let's take a closer look at what factors you should look at when buying a call option. It's not as simple as buying a call on a stock that is going up.

The Right Strike Price

As you know from our earlier discussions, understanding strike prices is the key to your success as an options trader. If you choose the wrong strike price, you could lose money, even if you're right about the direction and timing of the stock. So before you choose a strike price, you must take the time to think about the many factors that will lead you to a profitable call.

Out-of-the-Money Strike Price

Notice that the calls that are out-of-the-money are the cheapest. For example, looking at the option chain in Figure 9-1, it will only cost you $0.45 to buy the March 75 call. The April 80 is even cheaper—a bargain at $0.30. If you bought ten contracts representing 1,000 shares of this far out-of-the-money option, it would only cost you $300.

What are the chances that Boeing is going to hit $80 a share by April 22? That is the bet you'll make if you buy the April 80. When you look at the ask price, you see that the market doesn't think too highly of the chances. Keep this in mind: many (perhaps most) out-of-the-money calls expire unexercised.

Many people love buying out-of-the-money calls because they are not only cheaper but also provide the greater reward if the underlying stock explodes higher. Since trading options is a game of probabilities, you could say that the probability of an out-of-the-money call becoming profitable by the expiration date is slim, but not impossible. It's true that people make home runs on occasion, but don't confuse this with a trading strategy.

In-the-Money Strike Price

When you look at the ask price of the deep in-the-money May 65 call, it is a whopping $8.90 a contract (but this doesn't necessarily mean it's an unfair price). The near in-the-money March 70, however, is a more reasonable $3.30. If you go out another month, to April 70, the ask price is $4.20, while the May 70 is $4.90. As you will remember, the farther away the expiration date, the more the option costs.

As an option buyer, you have to weigh all of these factors before committing your money to the options market. In general, you'll probably want to buy in-the-money options. The reason involves many factors, all of which we'll explore next.

If your stock is at $73 a share, you could consider the 70 strike price. If your stock is at $75 a share, perhaps aim for the 72.50 strike price. The reason is this. When buying call options, the in-the-money strike prices won't erode as quickly as the out-of-the-money or at-the-money options. On the other hand, you probably don't want to buy too deep in-the-money calls as they are too expensive. The whole idea of options is to use less money.

Nevertheless, when you buy in-the-money calls, although the option costs more, you are paying for security and safety. Remember the old saying "You get what you pay for." Too many traders are lured into buying out-of-the-money calls because they are cheaper. Although $0.25 and $0.40 options are tempting, they are cheap for a reason. On the other hand, if you are purposely speculating, you can buy many more of the cheap options with the opportunity to double, triple, and quadruple your initial investment.

Another advantage of choosing an in-the-money call is that a moderate move in the underlying stock can still bring you profits.

Advanced Note: The pros have a name for this phenomenon. They call it delta, which will be discussed in Chapter 15.

One Rule of Thumb: Don't let price alone determine what calls to buy. This allows me to bring up one of my favorite quotes, from Oliver Wendell Holmes: "People know the price of everything but the value of nothing."

Here is something else to think about. If you are buying calls for the first time, you can start by buying in-the-money calls, but you have to experiment to determine which calls are most profitable.

Trying to Get the Best Price

When you are a call buyer, you will focus on the ask price. This is simply what the market believes is the fair price of the option. Although you want to pay a fair price, you should not always look for the lowest price. After all, the chances of making a substantial profit from cheap options are remote. Yet, many speculators willingly seek out the cheapest options, hoping for a home run.

Yes, home runs are possible; you can also win the lottery too. But if your goal is to be a consistently profitable trader, then chasing only after the cheapest options will likely be a money-losing proposition. In this case, you are gambling, not trading.

Tick-Tock: The Expiration Date

Unlike call sellers, time works against the call buyer. That tick-tock sound you hear is the sound of your option losing value. Call buyers are always concerned with how much time is left to expiration. As soon as you press the enter key, the clock is running. That is why it's so essential that you pay close attention to the expiration date. Options have a funny way of expiring before your option play had time to develop. Even if you are right about the direction of the underlying stock, you have to beat the strike price (plus the premium) or you won't make a dime.

So what expiration date should you choose? As you know, the farther away the expiration date, the more expensive the option. That makes sense. You are paying more money for the privilege of having more time for the underlying stock to rise in value.

For example, when you look at the option chain for Boeing in Figure 9-1, you see that you will have to pay $3.30 for the March 70 (one month away), while the April 70 is $4.20 each (two months away), and the May 70 is $4.90 (three months away).

In general, you should avoid choosing calls with the current month's expiration date because the time span is so short. Although out-of-the-money calls with short expiration dates are cheaper, it's unlikely they will be profitable. Most traders believe it's worth it to pay a bit more for an extra month's breathing room. The only exception would be if you know something explosive is going to happen to the underlying stock.

In general, if you are going to buy calls, it's probably best to buy an expiration date at least a month out. If it's November, then trade the December contracts. That gives you a balance between a reasonable price and enough time for the stock to make a move.

Important Rule: The closer the call option gets to the expiration date, the faster it loses value. That is why an option is called a wasting asset. Some refer to it as a melting ice cube.

What Is a Profitable Call?

After talking to professional traders as well as relying on my own personal experience and extensive research, the profile of a profitable call is clear (although there are exceptions). And the winner is....

. . . .
A profitable call = a relatively low premium with a strike price and expiration date that gives you the highest reward with the least amount of risk.
. . . .

Caveat: Once again, if you are an expert trader, you could find exceptions to what I consider a profitable call. But you have to start somewhere, and the above example is a good beginning. Your eventual goal, obviously, is to come up with your own criteria.

The Rise and Fall of Long-Term Capital Management

Options traders can learn a lot from the rise and fall of Long-Term Capital Management, a hedge fund run by a group of powerful and successful academics and traders who specialized in options and other derivatives.

The Rise

In 1994, John Meriwether, a former vice chairman and head of bond trading at Salomon Brothers, founded the hedge fund Long-Term Capital Management (LTCM). Other principals of the firm included some of the best and brightest financial minds in the world, including two Nobel prize–winning economists and a vice chairman of the Federal Reserve Board. The hedge fund began trading with over $1 billion in investor capital.

Large investment banks and other sophisticated investors eagerly invested approximately $1.3 billion in the hedge fund (the minimum investment was $10 million). LTCM was "destined for success," the financial media proclaimed. But there were some unusual rules. For example, because it was a hedge fund, it conducted its operations in secret. Nevertheless, for the first three years the fund had excellent, although not spectacular, returns.

Originally, the hedge fund created complex mathematical models that took advantage of price discrepancies between U.S., Japanese, and European government bonds. The "nondirectional" strategies it used also included profiting from merger takeovers. As its trading positions grew, LTCM took highly leveraged positions in index options such as the S&P 500, as well as stock options. At the beginning of 1998, the firm borrowed $125 billion with approximately $5 billion of equity. By any measurement, they were heavily leveraged.

The Fall

In 1998, LTCM began to unravel as its returns began to plummet. It started after the Russian government devalued the ruble on its government bonds. Soon, investors began to sell Japanese and European bonds to buy U.S. Treasury bonds. This was the unanticipated event that LTCM and its computer models didn't plan for. Instead of booking profits, LTCM started hemorrhaging money, creating a liquidity crisis.

By August, the hedge fund had lost $1.85 billion in capital as investors sought higher-quality bonds. Up to this point, the company had been highly successful, but many of its largest investors began to sell. As rumors spread, institutional investors nervously began to pull their money out, creating a full-fledged panic. Once investors got nervous, it started a vicious cycle of additional selling.

Alan Greenspan, chairman of the Federal Reserve Bank of New York, arranged a billion-dollar bailout for LTCM. When the accounts were cleared, the losses for LTCM totaled $4.6 billion, all in four months. Many banks simply wrote off millions of dollars in losses. A number of top executives at various banks resigned their positions for investing so heavily in LTCM.

What Went Wrong
After the collapse of LTCM, financial experts were able to take a closer look at the mistakes made by some of the smartest people in the investment world. Critics said that the LTCM hedge fund managers didn't take into account all the possible risks.

Although LTCM had access to the most sophisticated computers and formulas, the managers didn't plan for people acting irrationally when confronted with unanticipated events, such as a devalued ruble. In addition, its highly leveraged options positions caused their positions to unravel quickly when investors pulled their money.

Ironically, according to their computer models, LTCM thought their positions were low risk. Although the hedge fund managers were extremely bright, they didn't fully appreciate that they held such highly leveraged and risky positions.

Note: If you'd like to learn more about the rise and fall of LTCM, you will want to read *When Genius Failed* (Random House, 2001) by

Roger Lowenstein, which describes in page-turning detail the entire debacle. It is a good reminder that you should always plan for what could go wrong when trading stocks or options.

. . . .

Now that you know how to choose profitable call options, you will be introduced to one of the most fascinating but complex concepts in options trading: volatility and options pricing.

10

Volatility and Options Pricing

Even though I've told you that buying calls is relatively easy, I'm going to contradict myself and look under the hood of the car and see how the engine works, to use a popular analogy. It won't be long before you understand why trading options has a reputation for being challenging. (Some say this really is rocket science!) Although volatility and options pricing can be baffling at times, I will try to make these concepts understandable.

If you are serious about trading call options, however, it's essential for you to understand volatility and options pricing. For professional traders, their livelihood depends on understanding these concepts. The good news is once you have learned these concepts, you can apply them to all of the options strategies in this book. This will help make you a better trader and give you additional insights into the inner workings of the options market.

However, if you still don't comprehend them after reading this chapter, you can gain additional knowledge from my interview with options expert Sheldon Natenberg in Chapter 17.

What Factors Affect the Premium?

You shouldn't underestimate the importance of premium when buying or selling calls. In fact, you could spend years understanding the factors that affect an options premium, which is how much you will pay for an option (if buying) or how much you will receive (if selling). Although I touched on these factors when discussing covered calls, now I'll take a closer look. There are six major factors that directly affect options premiums. These include:

1. A change in the price of the underlying stock
2. The strike price
3. How much time is left until expiration
4. Interest rates
5. Dividends
6. Volatility of the underlying stock

I have previously discussed the importance of the strike price, the expiration date, and the underlying stock. Obviously, these three factors directly affect the option premium.

In addition, although interest rates and dividends indirectly affect the price of an option, they are not as obvious, which is why I won't discuss them in more depth. For now, keep in mind that when interest rates are low, more people and companies borrow money and buy stocks and options, which affect an option's price. When interest rates are high, it tends to cramp borrowing, which also affects options prices.

Before I discuss the sixth factor on the list, volatility, let's take a look at option pricing. It's not enough to simply know what you paid or received for an option. You also need to determine what an option is really worth. This is the only way you'll know if you are getting a fair deal. As you'll see later in this chapter, option traders use a variety of methods to determine whether they are paying a reasonable price.

What Is an Option Worth?

If you looked at the option premium, all you will learn is how much the option costs. But traders also want to know the true value of the option. After all, they don't want to overpay for the option. To help explain this further, let's look at the following formula.

Option Price (Premium) = Intrinsic Value + Time Value
$5.50 $5.00 $0.50

You have just learned that the option premium consists of two factors, intrinsic value and time value. The third factor, volatility, will be discussed later in this chapter. For now, I will explain intrinsic value and time value in more detail.

What Is Intrinsic Value?

When you look at an option price, the portion of the option that is in-the-money is intrinsic value. In other words, intrinsic value is how much the option is worth if you exercised it today. It is also the portion of the option that won't lose value because of the passage of time. Although in-the-money options have intrinsic value, out-of-the-money and at-the-money options have an intrinsic value of zero.

It's easy to calculate intrinsic value. For example, if IBM was currently at $81 a share and we bought the 80 strike price call, then the intrinsic value of the option is $1. It's simply the difference between the underlying stock and the strike price. Here is a formula to help you remember.

Stock Price – Strike Price = Intrinsic Value
$81 $80 $1

To give you another example, if a stock is trading at $33 and the strike price is $30, the intrinsic value is $3. It has intrinsic value of $3 no matter when it expires.

Therefore, when you hear traders say their options have intrinsic value, it simply means their options are worth something, which is another way of saying the option is in-the-money.

Important Fact: A stock that is in-the-money will be worth at least its intrinsic value. At-the-money and out-of-the-money options have no intrinsic value at all. They only have time value.

What Is Time Value?

You already know that as soon as you buy an option, time becomes your enemy. As the option gets closer to the expiration date, the option price begins to deteriorate rather rapidly because of a very important concept: time value (also called extrinsic value). Time value is simply what is left over after you have calculated intrinsic value. It is calculated based on how much time is left until expiration. For example, if the IBM call option costs $1.20 and the intrinsic value of the option is $1.00, the time value would be $0.20.

An option that is due in three months will have some time value, but an option due in one month will have less than a third time value left. During the last day of an option, there is hardly any time value left—there is only intrinsic value.

Remember when you sold covered calls in Chapter 4? With covered calls, time was on your side. It favored you, which is one of the advantages of being a seller. But as a call buyer, time works against you. As soon as you buy the call, the clock is ticking. As the expiration date approaches, the time value of the option deteriorates, and the option price drops in value.

Why is this? As the option approaches expiration, the underlying stock has less and less time to move in a favorable direction. There is less and less opportunity for the stock to move above the strike price as the expiration date approaches.

Therefore, if you buy an option with one month of time value, you'll have the greatest amount of depreciation. For example, if you bought a February options contract in February, every three or four days the option will erode quickly. On the other hand, if you bought an option with three months until expiration, it will still erode but not as quickly.

Important Note: One reason traders lose money even when they're right about the direction of the underlying stock is because of deteriorating time value.

The Mystery of Option Pricing

Now we'll get to the fun part. You are ready to buy a call option and calculate that the intrinsic value of your IBM option is $2 ($82 stock price – $80 strike price = $2 intrinsic value). There is a month left to expiration, so we'll estimate a time value of $0.90. When you look up the price of the option, you're assuming it will cost approximately $2.90.

Guess what? Instead of the $2.90 you thought you'd pay, you're surprised when the cost is $3.50. Why is it so expensive? Because there are several other variables included in the option price—for example, a very important and somewhat mysterious concept called *volatility*. Therefore, the option price will include a number of factors. Some of the premium will be intrinsic value, some will be time value, and some will be volatility.

To accurately calculate volatility, you need either an advanced degree in calculus, an understanding of options pricing models, or a good options calculator (I chose number 3). In fact, you could say that volatility is one of the most misunderstood but most important variables when pricing options.

I can explain volatility with a short answer or a long answer. The short answer uses Google as an example. A stock like Google is very volatile because it moves up and down like a yo-yo. Because it is so volatile, call buyers will pay more for it, knowing that there is a good chance the stock will reach the strike price before expiration.

Therefore, call buyers pay more for volatility, and the ask price of a volatile stock like Google will be more expensive. On the other hand, a stock like GE isn't volatile at all. Therefore, you won't pay extra for the volatility, so the option price will be much lower. For many of you, this is all you have to know about volatility.

Volatility: The X Factor

Now I'll give you the long answer.

When pricing options, volatility is one of the most important factors to consider (many pros say it is *the* most important factor). Unfortunately, although many traders mention volatility, few understand what it's really used for. At the most basic level, *volatility* means movement, as in how much the underlying stock or option moves within a certain amount of time. That's simple enough. But it's using the measurement of volatility to price options that is complex and confusing, relying on complicated statistical formulas.

Volatility is that very elusive factor that can cause you to lose money even when you are correct. For example, you could be right about the direction of the underlying stock. You could also be right about the timing. And yet, at the expiration date, you still lost money. Why? Because of volatility. Perhaps you paid so much for the pumped-up volatility that you ended up losing money.

There are two main types of volatility that options traders try to calculate: *historical* and *implied*. The other two types of volatility, *future* and *expected*, are harder to quantify and will not be discussed in this book.

Historical Volatility

Historical volatility, displayed as a percentage, measures how much a stock moves based on historical prices over a certain period. For example, the range for GE for the last six months is between $32 and $36. The greater the range of the stock price, the greater the volatility. In other words, the stock is more volatile and, in general, the option premiums will be more expensive.

If a stock moves no more than 2 or 3 percent within six months or a year, it has a low historical volatility. A stock that moves 20 or 30 percent in a year has higher historical volatility.

How does this information help you? People will often pay more money for options on volatile stocks with high historical volatility, which is why the option prices are so high on volatile stock options. Also remember that the higher the volatility, the greater the risk that the stock will go down, as well as the greater the potential return.

People often make decisions based on historical data even though they don't realize that's what they are doing. When you are trying to predict the future, the first thing you do is look at the past. Why? Because most of us believe that the past repeats itself.

Implied Volatility

Understanding implied volatility is not easy, even for the pros, so don't worry if you don't get it the first time. I certainly didn't. To demonstrate how difficult it is to define, I'd like you to answer a question. Can you define gravity for me? It's not too easy to explain, right? If you are a scientist, the most precise way to define gravity is through complicated scientific formulas using standard deviation. It's the same with implied volatility.

Without getting too scientific, *implied volatility* is simply what the market implies the option is worth. Unlike historical volatility, which can be graphed, implied volatility is more like a real-time indicator of how much the market is willing to pay for the option.

Another way to think of implied volatility is the feeling of urgency that traders have about certain stocks and options. Because of this urgency, you'll see higher implied volatility in some options.

Generally, stocks like Google had very high implied volatility— and might today. You can sense this urgency before an earnings release or some other important announcement. Guess what? Google options were expensive because of its high implied volatility. On the other hand, the lack of urgency in stocks and options like GE typically means lower implied volatility. You'll find that the options contracts on low implied volatility stocks like GE are cheaper. There isn't the same demand for these options.

The pros want to calculate implied volatility because they don't want to pay more for an option than they have to. For instance, if the implied volatility of a call or put is too high, then the option could be viewed as overpriced. You'll end up paying much more than the option is worth.

Professional options traders use complicated formulas that calculate implied volatility. Fortunately, there is software that will give you the implied volatility figures. This software is based on the revolutionary options pricing model, *Black-Scholes* (discussed in more detail in Chapter 16). You enter a number of parameters (for example, stock price, strike price, interest rate, dividends, and expiration date) into the model, and it will help calculate volatility levels, from low to high, and estimate or forecast how volatile the option will be until the expiration date.

In addition, options with higher implied volatility sometimes have a higher bid-ask spread. The spread on a stock option like GE might be $0.10 whereas the spread on an option with high implied volatility will be higher, for example, $0.30 or $0.40. In order to get into the profit zone, your option must first pass through the wider spread.

Generally, if you are buying calls, you are looking for underlying stocks that are more exciting than GE but maybe not as volatile as

Google. A stock like GE is an ideal candidate for a covered call, but perhaps not for speculative call buying. And with options that have a higher implied volatility, you are probably paying extra.

For example, the Irish biopharmaceutical company, Elan (NYSE: ELN), was waiting for the U.S. Food and Drug Administration (FDA) to approve a drug to treat multiple sclerosis. When the final decision is made by the FDA, the stock is going to move in one direction or another.

You plug in the data into the Black-Scholes pricing model for the Elan April 12.5 call option contract. The result? The April 12.5 call contract has an implied volatility of 162 percent. This means that this option is priced for a huge move, either up or down, until the expiration date. By the way, there is a 66 percent chance that the calculation is correct.

How does it help to know the implied volatility? First, the Elan April 12.5 call is technically overpriced at $2.15 per contract, pumped up with extremely high implied volatility. Fifty percent or lower implied volatility is more reasonable, while 100 percent is rather high. In Elan's case, an implied volatility of 162 percent is extreme. Nevertheless, it didn't stop options traders from scooping up the March and April call options for Elan. Figure 10-1 shows the open interest in these call options. As you can see, there is a lot of interest.

There are several option plays you can make. First, you can decide not to make the trade, knowing you are technically overpaying for that higher implied volatility.

ELN			ELAN CP PLC ADR				
:t	12.50	↑	-0.31	Bid	12.45	Size	5
						Calls	
Symbol	Date - Strike	Last	Change	Bid	Ask		Open Int
-ELNCB	Mar 18 06 10.00	$3.30	-$0.20	$3.20	$3.30		39601
-ELNCC	Mar 18 06 15.00	$0.65	-$0.15	$0.65	$0.75		55026
-ELNDB	Apr 22 06 10.00	$3.60	-$0.10	$3.50	$3.70		47169
-ELNDV	Apr 22 06 12.50	$2.15	-$0.10	$2.05	$2.15		50783
-ELNDC	Apr 22 06 15.00	$1.10	-$0.10	$1.05	$1.10		70488
-ELNDW	Apr 22 06 17.50	$0.45	-$0.15	$0.45	$0.50		34933
-ELNDD	Apr 22 06 20.00	$0.25	-$0.05	$0.20	$0.25		30943
-ELNDX	Apr 22 06 22.50	$0.10	-$0.05	$0.05	$0.10		30565

Figure 10-1   Open Interest

Source: Fidelity Investments. Copyright 2002 FMR Corp. All rights reserved.

Second, you could speculate by purchasing what you calculate as a high price for the April 12.5 at-the-money call option. Maybe you think it still has room to move on the upside if the FDA approves the drug. It's a bit of a gamble because you know the stock could go in either direction, up or down. Third, you could do what many pros do. They call it *buying volatility*. This means they buy options based on the movement of the option, not on the direction. As long as Elan makes a strong move in one direction or the other, the pros can make money. To learn how to make this play, you'll have to wait until Chapter 15, where I discuss straddles, an advanced options strategy.

Entire books have been written about the importance of volatility when pricing options, including Sheldon Natenberg's book *Option Volatility & Pricing: Advanced Trading Strategies and Techniques* (McGraw-Hill, 1994). The main reason I decided to interview Mr. Natenberg is that understanding volatility is extremely important, especially for professionals who trade for a living. Retail traders should obviously be aware of the effect of volatility on option prices.

If you want to calculate implied volatility, go to the Web site of the Options Industry Council (OIC), www.888options.com. Other Web sites have calculators based on the Black-Scholes pricing model. You have a choice of two options calculators: basic or advanced. After entering the variables, the calculator will give you an implied volatility percentage for the option.

Hint: There are also calculators that give you the historical volatility of the underlying stock. By comparing the historical volatility of the stock with the implied volatility of the option, you possibly have another way of determining if the option is overpriced.

Who Are Market Makers?

Market makers are individuals or firms that are obligated to buy and sell listed options during the trading day. It is a market maker's job to provide liquidity in the marketplace. For example, if there are more sell orders than buy orders, the market maker will step in and buy up the balance. The main job of the market maker is to keep the market moving or flowing in order to maintain a "fair and orderly market."

Options are traded at six exchanges, either on the floor of the exchange or electronically from off the floor. The six participant exchanges are the American Stock Exchange (AMEX), Chicago Board Options Exchange (CBOE), International Securities Exchange (ISE), Pacific Exchange (PCX), Philadelphia Stock Exchange (PHLX), and Boston Stock Exchange (BSE).

The market makers who trade options on the floor of the CBOE in Chicago are called *floor traders*. They yell and scream the bid and ask prices (the open outcry method). They want to be heard so they can fulfill the trade at a competitive price. Options are also traded off the floor with computers, matching buyers and sellers automatically.

As is the case with any trade, there must be someone on the other side, either to buy or sell. If you buy an option, someone is the seller. That someone might be the market maker. If you want to sell an option, the market maker will actually buy it from you, even if there is no seller available. They are literally "making a market" for the option.

Market makers have no choice. They *have* to make a market in every underlying stock that they trade in. So, if everyone's selling, they have to post a bid price. Keep in mind that although market makers are obliged to maintain liquidity in the market, they are not required to take a loss. In other words, if there is a transaction that isn't immediately profitable, market makers might rapidly replace that position with another option or a stock trade.

To get paid for the risks they are taking, market makers maintain a *spread* on each stock or option that they cover. For example, market makers might buy 10 IBM call contracts from you for $1.00 (the ask price) and then "offer" to sell it to another buyer for $1.05 (the bid price). The market makers keep the $0.05 difference *if* they can quickly find a $1.05 buyer. If they can't find a buyer immediately, they'll offset their position with another stock or option. When you add up the millions of shares that are traded each day, the potential profits could really add up.

Unlike individual traders, market makers won't usually hold options until expiration. In fact, they rarely hold options longer than a few *minutes*. They'll buy a covered call from you and immediately turn around and sell it to someone else or sell stock. Market makers do not like stagnant markets. After all, it doesn't help them if the market freezes up. If there isn't any trading, they don't make any money.

If you think that you can beat the market makers at their game, then listen to what one of my trading friends says. "Because of the spread, the market makers will always get their cut, which is the difference between the bid and ask price. Remember that although the market makers are obligated to take the other side of the transaction, they are not obligated to make a bad deal. In other words, they will buy the option you are selling but will give it to you at the price they want, not the price you want." He added that no one is smarter than the market and almost no one is smarter than the market makers.

There is a lot you can learn from market makers. First, market makers have no preconceived opinion of the market. They follow the volume and direction of the market but don't try to predict which direction the market is going. Second, they pay attention to the market all day long. Even if they go to lunch, they are usually watching their position. Therefore, if you want to trade stocks or options full-time, it will be helpful if you acquire the focus and discipline of professional market makers.

Many people think market makers compete with the retail trader. On the contrary, market makers are not concerned with your relatively small 10-lot option orders. What they watch out for are the 500-lot orders (representing 50,000 shares of the underlying stock) from professional traders or computer programmed trades.

━━━━━━━━━━━━━━━━━━━━━━━━━━━━━━━━━

· ·

Now that you have been introduced to the concepts of volatility and pricing, you're ready to learn the mechanics of buying call options.

11

Step-by-Step: Buying Calls

If you got through the last chapter without too much difficulty, you're doing great. Learning how to price options and determine profitability are extremely challenging concepts, even for the experts. And even if you didn't completely understand these concepts, at least you've been introduced to them and can always review them later.

Meanwhile, the exciting part is actually signing on to the brokerage firm's Web site and buying call options. As I've said before, brokerage firms have invested millions of dollars in making it easy to buy and sell options.

Before we get to the mechanics of buying calls, however, I'll discuss some of the risks. Once again, I'm not trying to talk you out of this strategy; I only want to make you aware of the potential pitfalls. By being aware of the potential risks of using any options strategy, you will know exactly how to protect yourself in worst-case scenarios.

The Risks of Buying Calls

There are actually a number of risks when buying calls, which is why it's considered a speculative strategy. As I mentioned before, most options contracts expire unexercised by the expiration date. Although the exact figure is hard to estimate, I can confidently say that many speculators lose money. Of course, some traders have scored big in the options market, but many have not.

Perhaps you bought this book because you're looking for quick money without too much risk. That is how many people get lured into the options market (or any market, for that matter). I've been to options seminars where the instructors incorrectly said that buying calls is a "guaranteed investment," allowing you to make "consistent income." First, there is nothing consistent or guaranteed about buying calls. And second, you should know that the odds are against you from the beginning.

Nevertheless, as long as you are fully aware of the risks, there is nothing wrong with speculating on occasion. As always, knowledge (and discipline) can help you avoid making mistakes and losing money. What is the biggest risk to trading calls? The answer is simple. You could lose the entire amount you paid for the contract. At least you won't lose more than you paid, and perhaps less than if you bought stock.

Although the mechanics of buying calls is simple, many people underestimate the skill it takes to be successful. Unfortunately, many people don't take the time to study and research. They are looking for the quick score, and the truth is that occasionally people do get lucky. As an options trader, however, you don't want to depend on luck to be successful.

In addition, some people make huge paper gains but fail to realize how quickly profits can disappear. Once again, the problem is that people aren't fully aware of the speculative nature of call options. In the options market, if you don't move quickly, you could lose your entire investment.

Another problem with buying calls is that you have to be right on two counts: the timing and the direction. That is, if you are right about the direction of the underlying stock but it doesn't move before the expiration date, you will lose money. And if the stock doesn't move in the right direction, you will lose money, perhaps your entire investment (although it's a fraction of the cost of a stock investment). And finally, because the pros at the exchanges or in their home offices have the most expensive software and make a career from trading, you are at a disadvantage. Although it's possible to make a profitable living buying and selling options, it's not easy. For example, some people think that buying calls is similar to buying a lottery ticket. They think that all they need to hit the jackpot is the right software that will find the winning options combination.

Rule: You should not use the options market (or any market) as a substitute for gambling, although many people do; compulsive gamblers, in fact, are drawn to this market because of the action. More often than not, they lose money, usually because the options expire before they were proved correct (or so they say).

Now that you are fully aware of the risks of buying calls, I will introduce you to a word you learned in the previous chapter: the spread. Understanding spreads is essential when you calculate how much you made or lost on an options trade.

The Power of the Spread

The *spread*, the difference between the bid and ask price, directly affects how much money you'll make on a trade. If you buy options, you want to pay a fair price for the option. So what is a fair price? Probably somewhere in between the bid price and ask price. Although measured in pennies, the spread still takes money out of your pocket (especially if you were to immediately liquidate your position). When trading *stocks*, the spread is often small enough (on a percentage basis) to be ignored. When trading *options*, however, the spreads can be rather significant.

Because of the spread, you immediately start off with a loss when buying calls (the spread is irrelevant when you sell covered calls). For example, if the bid price is $1.00 and the ask price is $1.10, you are probably going to pay $1.10. (perhaps $1.05 if you're fortunate.) If you turned around to sell it for $1.00, you would be looking at a 9 percent loss. That is the power of the spread, which is the dime the market maker would like to collect. Obviously, you are hoping that the value of the option moves high enough to erase your initial loss.

Although $0.10 doesn't sound like much, in percentage terms it's rather substantial. So how do you manage a 9 or 10 percent loss right from the beginning? Although most call buyers have extremely positive attitudes, you'll have to work hard to overcome this disadvantage.

If you notice that the spread on your call or put option is greater than 30 cents, it is a warning—a red flag. Although you still could be right about the timing and direction of the stock, you still could lose money on the spread.

For example, if the bid is $1 and the ask price is $1.30, you are already behind by 30 percent. One of the threats to your trade is a loss in the spread, which is why you need to watch it carefully. The spread changes all the time, and if volatility rises on the option, the spread will widen. By the way, this is another reason why it's often difficult to trade options on volatile stocks.

Bottom Line: Pay close attention to the spread when buying calls or puts.

What to Expect from Buying Calls

Figure 11-1 is a visual representation of the risks and rewards of buying calls. The advantage of buying calls is that your profit potential is unlimited whereas your losses are limited. Only you can decide if this strategy makes sense for you and will help you with what you are trying to achieve.

Before You Place Your First Trade

Even with all of these risks and caveats, it's essential that you learn how to buy call options. If I didn't believe that, I never would have written this book. Now that you are aware of advantages and disadvantages of using this strategy, let's get started. The following screens will give you step-by-step instructions on how to buy calls.

In the option chain, you have already looked up the option symbol, strike price, and expiration date. In fact, before you place the order, you should know well in advance exactly what call you are buying.

If you're uncomfortable placing your own trade at first, you can ask the brokerage representatives for help. Once again, the most

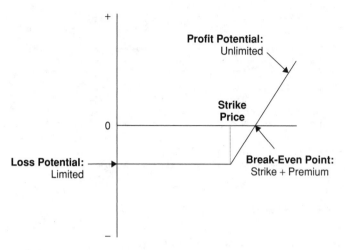

Figure 11-1   Risks and Rewards of Buying Calls
Source: CBOE. Copyright 2006. All rights reserved.

common mistake in trading is carelessness: entering the wrong symbols or prices.

What about Treasury Bills?

You might wonder what a paragraph about Treasury bills is doing in an options book. Before you place an options trade (or any trade, for that matter), you should ask yourself one question. Will I make more money investing in a Treasury bill (or other fixed-income product) or buying this call? The pros compare their trades to a specific benchmark, and you can do the same.

> *Hint*: Many individuals keep a portion of their portfolio in a core account such as fixed-income, and trade stocks or options in another account.

BA		BOEING CO						
Last		72.69	↓	-1.44	Bid	72.51	Size	1
							Calls	
Trade	Symbol	Date - Strike	Last	Change	Bid	Ask	Open Int	
Trade	**-BACN**	Mar 18 06 70.00	$3.30	-$1.10	$3.20	$3.30	3501	
Trade	**-BACV**	Mar 18 06 72.50	$1.50	-$1.30	$1.35	$1.45	51	
Trade	**-BACO**	Mar 18 06 75.00	$0.40	-$0.45	$0.40	$0.45	5358	
Trade	**-BADN**	Apr 22 06 70.00	$4.00	-$0.70	$4.00	$4.20	55	
Trade	**-BADV**	Apr 22 06 72.50	$2.45	-$0.95	$2.40	$2.50	220	
Trade	**-BADO**	Apr 22 06 75.00	$1.30	-$0.55	$1.25	$1.35	437	

Figure 11-2   Option Chain: Boeing Calls
Source: Fidelity Investments. Copyright 2002 FMR Corp. All rights reserved.

Let's Begin Trading!

Figure 11-2 is the call option chain for Boeing.
Here are some observations:

1. The current quote on Boeing is $72.69.
2. The call option symbol we are interested in buying is BACN, the March 70 call, an option that is in-the-money by approximately 2 points.
3. The expiration date is almost a month away.
4. The ask price is $3.30. You should also notice that the spread is $0.10, the difference between the $3.20 bid price and the $3.30 ask price.

For only $330, you are controlling 100 shares of Boeing stock that are worth over $7,000. This is the power of leverage that I mentioned earlier—and the reason people like buying calls. The underlying stock, Boeing, will have to move well past the strike price of $70 for you to make a profit. In this case, you only have a month.

Note: You could have bought the April 70 for $4.20, which would have given you an extra month of time but would have cost $0.90 more. These are the kinds of decisions that call buyers have to make all the time.

Figure 11-3 displays a sample option entry screen for buying calls. The screen on your brokerage account may look different from the one displayed here.

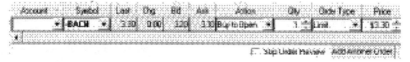

Figure 11-3 Call Option Entry Screen
Source: Fidelity Investments. Copyright 2002 FMR Corp.

Account Name or Number

If you have more than one account, be sure the correct account is entered.

ACTION: *You enter the account number or name.*

Symbol

Once again, be sure you enter the correct symbol, and it wouldn't hurt to double-check your entry. Some brokerage firms require you to enter a special symbol like a dash before the quote.

ACTION: *You enter the option symbol.*

Last, Change, Bid, and Ask Price

The option's last sale price, how much it changed, and the current bid and ask price are automatically displayed for you. Because you are buying calls, you will focus primarily on the ask price, which is probably how much you will pay for the option.

Note: Once again, don't pay much attention to the last sale price, as it could be five seconds ago, five minutes ago, or five days ago.

Buy to Open

In Figure 11-4, you need to select the correct options transaction.

Account	Symbol	Last	Chg.	Bid	Ask	Action	Qty	Order Type	Price
▼	-BACN ▼	3.30	0.00	3.20	3.30	Buy to Open ▼	1 ‡	Limit ▼	$3.30 ‡

Figure 11-4   Buy to Open Order Entry
Source: Fidelity Investments. Copyright 2002 FMR Corp. All rights reserved.

Let's review the four choices you have when buying or selling options. You must become very familiar with these terms before you can successfully trade options.

Buy to Open: Select this when buying calls or puts. It's used to initiate or create a long position.

Sell to Close: Select this when you are closing out or selling a call or put that you have previously bought.

Sell to Open: Select this when you are selling calls or puts, including selling covered calls. (Most often used to initiate a covered call position.)

Buy to Close: Select this when you are closing out or decreasing a call or put position that you have previously sold. You also select this when you want to close a covered call position prior to expiration.

Since you are buying calls, you will select Buy to Open, because in option terminology, you have just opened up a position to buy a call.

ACTION: *You select Buy to Open.*

Quantity

Because you are buying 1 contract (representing 100 shares of the underlying stock), you enter the number "1." Once again, the most common mistake is entering the number of shares instead of the number of contracts. For example, if you enter 100 contracts, it will be similar to buying 10,000 shares of the underlying stock. Obviously, you don't want to make that mistake.

ACTION: *You enter 1 contract for 100 shares. (Most people never enter more than 10 contracts at one time.)*

Symbol	Last	Chg.	Bid	Ask	Action	Qty	Order Type	Price
▼ -BACN ▼	3.31	0.00	0.00	0.00	Buy to Open ▼	1	▼	

Market
Limit
☐ Skip Order Pre Stop Loss | ther Order

Figure 11-5 Market or Limit Order
Source: Fidelity Investments. Copyright 2002 FMR Corp. All rights reserved.

Order Type: Market or Limit Order

In Figure 11-5, you need to choose between a market order or limit order.

When you are trading options, it's recommended that you select Limit order, meaning that you select the price at which you'll buy the call. You let the brokerage firm work the order to try and get you the best price. If you select Market order, on the other hand, you are letting the market determine your price. The advantage of a market order is in the speed of the fill, although you might not get the price you anticipate.

ACTION: *You select Limit order.*

Price

Using the Boeing call example in Figure 11-2 (BACN), the bid price is $3.20 and the ask price is $3.30. But it may change by the time you're ready to place the order. More than likely, you will be selecting the current ask price, but you can try and shave off a nickel to try to obtain the most competitive price. At the very least, you can enter a price you think is fair. There is always a chance the market will meet your price (but there are never any guarantees).

If you do enter the current limit price, you will probably be filled quickly. Some traders enter the bid price as their limit order, but it's unlikely you'll get filled unless the underlying stock drops in price.

ACTION: *Enter the current ask price of $3.30.*

The brokerage firm will try to get a price of $3.30 per contract or better. When the order is filled, a $330 net debit will show up in your account. This is the total cost of buying one contract, not including commissions.

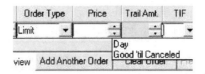

Figure 11-6   Time Limit

Time Limit

Once again, if you are trading options, you will select Day, which means that the order must be filled by the end of the day or it will be canceled. (See Figure 11-6.) If you select a competitive price, more than likely the order will be filled in a timely manner.

Type of Account

You only have a choice if you have both an IRA and a regular brokerage account. (See Figure 11-7.) If you have a brokerage account, it'll probably be designated as a margin account.

ACTION: *Select Margin account (only if you have multiple accounts). Otherwise, you won't have to do anything.*

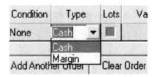

Figure 11-7   Type of Account

Preview Your Order

If there is a preview button, double-check your order before you press the enter key. In the preview screen, the commission and the total cost of the order are usually displayed. This is your last chance to make any changes before the order is filled. You'd be amazed at the number of careless errors that people make. Take the time to check your order or you could lose money.

Broker Instructions: If you called your broker and wanted to place the above order by phone, you would say, "I want to buy one call for Boeing March 70 for a limit price of $3.30 (or better) good for the day only."

Note: If you do decide to place a call with a broker, the recorded telephone call is a valid contract. Be sure to speak clearly and use options terminology to place the trade.

Press the Enter Key

When you press the enter key, the order will be routed to the options exchange. A seller will be matched to your buy order. The net debit will immediately appear in your account. Congratulations! You have bought your first call. You can't relax, however, because you need to closely monitor your option position.

Advanced Note: Before you press the enter key, you should be aware of *splits, mergers, acquisitions,* and other corporate actions that will do odd things to your options positions. You'll need to do further research on how to handle "adjustments" made to your options because of outside events. By the way, these options are loosely referred to as *adjusted options.* Hint: Check to make sure you're not buying one of the adjusted options.

Do Most Options Really Expire Worthless?

One of the most widely quoted statistics about the options market is that "90 percent of options contracts expire worthless." It reminds me of the joke that 85 percent of statistics are made up. Before you nod your head in agreement, you can enter any number you want. Nevertheless, I wanted to take a closer look at this statistic to see if it's really true or a misleading myth.

Note: The term, expire worthless, although grammatically incorrect, is often used by options traders to describe what happens to options on the expiration date.

First, although critics of the options market continue to claim that 90 percent of options contracts expire worthless, the CBOE (and other experts) say the figure is closer to 50 percent. Perhaps one of the problems is that people aren't always talking about the same strategy.

For example, if you are using a covered call strategy, you *want* the options you sold to expire worthless. In fact, if the options you sold weren't exercised, your strategy was successful and profitable. If you are using the very popular covered call strategy, although many options expire worthless, it doesn't mean the call seller lost money (as long as the stock didn't drop).

Buying call and put options is another matter, however. Because this can be a speculative strategy, it's very likely that many (although the exact percentage is hard to pin down) call options expire worthless by the expiration date. And don't forget that the whole idea of options is that they eventually expire.

Nevertheless, you can say with some confidence that many speculators who trade options lose money. An even more accurate statement would be that most call and put options expire unused or *unexercised* by the expiration date. Whether it's 50 percent or 90 percent, only the people who trade them know for sure. It's also obvious that this figure changes depending on the date and type of contract. For example, options on stock might have different results than options on indexes.

In summary, it is misleading and inaccurate to make a blanket statement that 90 percent of options contracts expire worthless. It seems accurate, however, to say that many call or put options expire unexercised by the expiration date. (I can't say for sure whether they expire worthless or not.) All that really matters is whether your trade is profitable.

Caveat: The entire issue of worthless options is a controversial subject with many options traders. Everyone seems to have an opinion and the facts to support their view. My goal, on the other hand, is simply to point out the issue and let the experts determine who is right. In the future, I'm sure there will be reports and studies that will shed light on or perhaps make this issue even more confusing.

Now that you've learned the mechanics of buying calls, you will next learn how to manage and maintain your call position.

12

Managing Your Call Position

The easy part about buying calls is placing the order. In this chapter, you will do the hard part: managing your call position. That is when you are feeling the most hopeful. Perhaps you have already calculated how much money you are going to make (always a bad sign). There are so many choices of what you can do, which is why you have to keep close track of the underlying stock as well as the option.

As you remember in Chapter 7, it is essential that you create a trading plan before and after you place your first options trade. A trading plan is a road map that helps you to determine when to enter or exit an option position.

The following is a sample trading plan for buying calls.

Your Trading Plan

As the call buyer, you are in control of the right to buy the stock until the expiration date. This is why you need to monitor the position so closely. After you press the enter key, the underlying stock has only three ways to move: up, down, or sideways.

To refresh your memory, you bought call options on the Boeing March 70 call option, BACN. The ask price you had previously entered was $3.30.

Note: You must keep a close eye on both the underlying stock and option if you want to make a profitable trade. The underlying stock will help determine the direction of the call. Remember that wherever the underlying stock goes, your option will probably follow (although there are exceptions).

The Underlying Stock Moves Down

Outcome: The stock falls, dropping below the strike price.

What to expect: This is not what you wanted. As the underlying stock falls, watch as the option price deteriorates. As the stock falls below the strike price, the option will eventually lose value and become worthless. The time value of the option deteriorates rapidly with only weeks left until expiration.

Analysis: As the clock counts down, it is very likely your option will expire worthless by the expiration date. If a stock moves in the wrong direction, you have a number of choices. First, if there is still time left and you don't think the stock will make a dramatic turnaround, you could try to salvage what is left of the contract by selling the entire position.

Remember that it's hard for underlying stocks that are below the strike price to become profitable (once in the cellar, they tend to stay there). By the time one week is left, you might as well hold on to your nearly worthless call options (but that is a decision only you can make).

At this point, you have little to lose by holding the position until the expiration date, hoping for a miracle. Occasionally, a few days before expiration, call options have been known to explode higher. By the way, if the option does expire worthless, you don't have to do anything. You were already debited for the cost of the option, so your account doesn't change.

To Sell (or Close) Your Position

If you do decide to sell at a loss, you will go to the brokerage screen and select *Sell to Close*. This means you are selling to close the position. You mark it as a bad trade and learn from your mistake.

Broker Instructions: If you called your broker and wanted to place the above order by phone, you would say, "I want to sell to close all open contracts on Boeing at the market price."

Note: This assumes you have multiple contracts and multiple expirations.

The Underlying Stock Stays the Same

Outcome: The stock stays at or near the strike price.

What to expect: This is not an ideal situation. If the underlying stock doesn't move, the option will begin to lose value, especially as it gets closer to expiration.

Analysis: You know that if the stock doesn't move very much by the expiration date, your option will probably expire with lesser value.

Hint: This is the time you might think of salvaging what little gain you have. If you believe the stock could make a dramatic turnaround, by all means hold your position. At least with stocks that are near the strike price, you are closer to profitability than you are with stocks that are below the strike price.

Advanced Hint: You can also *roll over* to a later expiration date.

The Underlying Stock Moves Up

Outcome: The stock moves above the strike price.

What to expect: This is exactly what you want and expect. As the underlying stock moves up, watch as the option price jumps. The longer and higher the stock moves above the strike price, the more valuable the call option will become. By the expiration date, although time value has disappeared, the option still has intrinsic value.

Analysis: You have a number of choices when the underlying stock is higher than the strike price. The more it moves higher, the more valuable the option will become. Although many people think it's easy to manage a winning position, it's actually quite challenging. With options, you have many choices for what to do next.

Because of the fickle nature of the options market, it's always a good idea to take money off the table and book profits when you have gains. If the underlying stock moves up too much and your profits are so high that you are giving high fives to your friends and family, think about selling immediately.

Therefore, if the stock is above the strike price (and your call option is in-the-money), you can sell the call on or before the expiration date and book the profits. You select *Sell to Close* on your brokerage screen to close out the option position. Your profit is the difference between what you paid for the option ($3.30) and what the option is selling for now.

You have another choice and that is to exercise the option and buy the underlying stock. Perhaps the main reason you would exercise the option is because you believe the stock will continue to go up. Do you remember at what price you exercise the option? The answer is at the strike price. If you do decide to exercise the option, there are certain steps you are required to take.

To Exercise Your Call Option

First, you *must* notify your brokerage firm (preferably by phone) whether you plan to exercise your call option. You should let them know at least 24 hours before the brokerage firm's cutoff time on Expiration Friday. (New Rule: Any option that is in-the-money by $0.05 or greater at expiration will be automatically exercised.)

Many call buyers wait until the expiration date to exercise their option, but American-style options can technically be exercised at anytime. Once the option is exercised, however, the exercise is irrevocable.

If you do decide to exercise, the seller will be ordered to deliver the shares of stock, where the shares will appear (after a three-day settlement period) in your account by Saturday at noon. Your account will be debited for the purchase price (i.e., the strike price).

A Strategy for Selling Covered Calls

If you think about it, after exercising the call option and purchasing the stock at the strike price, you could turn around and sell covered calls on the stock. This works best for rising stocks that have slowed down. The ability to sell covered calls on the underlying stock is another reason why exercising an option can make sense.

Advanced Call Strategies

Some of the strategies described below will give you other ideas about using options to increase your returns.

Rolling Up

We discussed rolling up in the covered call section. Nevertheless, you can do the same with call options. To review, rolling up a call means you close out your current position and roll it up to a later strike price.

For example, let's say you paid a dollar for a call for an underlying stock selling for $20 a share. The stock is now at $23 a share at expiration, and the call is worth $3. Instead of exercising the option, you sell the option for a profit, and buy next month's call: the 25 strike price selling for $2 a contract. You are basically using the profit from the first call and rolling up to buy the next strike price. It works best when a stock is "on a roll."

Roll Over

The roll over (also known as a roll forward or roll out) was also discussed in Part Two. To review, when you roll over an option, it means you exchange the option for a later expiration date. The strike price remains the same, but the expiration date changes. For example, you close the March contract and open an April contract.

Arbitrage

There are times when you might see a disparity between the stock price and the option price. In other words, you are looking for options that are undervalued compared to the selling price of a stock. During those times, the options market doesn't fully realize the value of the stock. Therefore, the option is undervalued compared to the selling price of a stock. This is what the pros call arbitrage, when you take advantage of price discrepancies between two securities. On occasion, you can find arbitrage opportunities in the options market.

For example, a few years ago there was breaking news about Dell computer after the stock price had already risen 10 points. The call options, however, barely moved. Obviously, the market had not priced the Dell options correctly. Therefore, if you moved quickly and bought 10 calls on Dell, less than an hour later your calls would have been worth substantially more. By that time, the options were priced correctly, reflecting the increase in the Dell stock.

Keep in mind it takes a lot of work and monitoring to find these arbitrage opportunities. They are not something you see on a daily basis. They usually result from a mathematical disparity rather than from breaking news. However, in the options market, anything can happen, so be on the lookout for these arbitrage opportunities.

The Tale of a Trader

As mentioned in Chapter 3, one of my friends, Daniel (not his real name), made $130,000 in three days, trading options. His roller-coaster ride started a week before when he received a tip from his stockbroker about a small California drug company whose stock was rumored to move much higher. According to the broker, the company, Hollis Eden Pharmaceuticals (Nasdaq: HEPH), was going to receive a multi-million-dose order of its newly developed antiradiation drug from the U.S. government. The government was supposed to announce its intentions by September 30, 2005.

After doing some basic fundamental research on the company, Daniel was convinced his broker was right. Daniel was looking for a home run, and a play like this didn't come along very often. The stock was trading for about $7.50 a share. Daniel's initial target price was $10 a share with a possible target of $30 a share (or so he hoped).

So with the broker's blessing, Daniel bought approximately 500 call contracts (controlling roughly 50,000 shares of stock) with multiple expiration dates and strike prices. The cheapest out-of-the-money calls were about $0.50 each.

By any standard, this was a huge bet on one stock. Many traders buy no more than 10 calls at a time. As it turned out, the broker was initially right. The stock went up over 34 percent before the anticipated announcement date. The call contract went from $0.50 to more than $2.80 on the expectation that the government would purchase a large quantity of the new drug.

I saw Daniel at the local coffee shop when he told me he was up over $130,000 in paper profits. He was giving high fives to his friends. This was the best one-day gain he had ever made in his life. This is the home run that all call buyers dream about.

Although I was glad to hear about his good fortune, I did ask him one question: "Did you sell?"

He looked at me with a slightly annoyed look. "I thought about it," he said. "But the announcement is coming out on Friday." You could see that look in his eye. "And the news is going to be good!" In his mind, it would be crazy to sell after such a large gain when a bigger gain was around the corner.

The next day, Thursday, September 29, he had second thoughts about his huge gains. He thought about selling the profitable calls to finance buying new calls. He even discussed it with his broker but never placed or confirmed the order.

Friday morning, the announcement was made on HEPH. Here is a paragraph from an article in the *Washington Post* (October 4, 2005): "On Friday, the company learned to its dismay that the government proposed to buy only 20,000 to 200,000 doses of this type of drug—not nearly enough to make final development economically feasible. The company's stock dropped sharply on the news, and some on Capitol Hill worried that the BioShield program—which has been in trouble because large drug companies have generally declined to participate—was headed for even rougher waters."

A picture is worth a thousand words. Figure 12-1 tells it all.

When the stock crumbled, so did all of Daniel's profits. In retrospect, Daniel learned several lessons: First, he vowed never

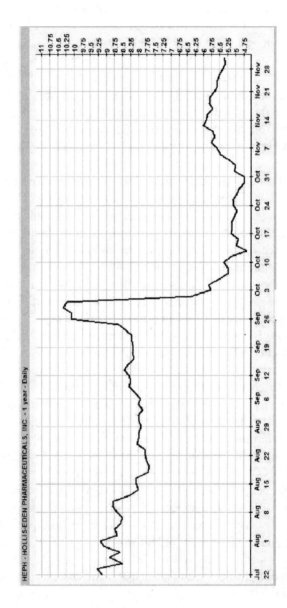

Figure 12-1   HEPH Chart

Source: Fidelity Investments. Copyright 2002 FMR Corp. All rights reserved.

to get so greedy (always easier said than done). He also vowed to take control of his buying and selling decisions and not leave them completely with the stockbroker. Ultimately, it's the responsibility of the client to tell the broker when and what to sell. Now you know why all calls to the brokerage firm are recorded.

By the way, when I ran into Daniel recently, he had just placed another order with his broker to buy more call options on HEPH (although not as many as before). This is quite common; some traders, after losing money on a stock or option, take it personally and want revenge. Once you get emotional over a stock, the market will probably beat you, which is exactly what happened to Daniel after he placed his second order. For the next three months, HEPH never went higher than $6 a share. For the second time, his call options expired worthless.

* *

Now that you've been introduced to buying calls, you're going to learn how to buy puts, another speculative strategy. Once again, it's essential that you learn this strategy, even if you never decide to use it. By the way, you might want to take a break before moving to Part Four. There is a big difference between buying calls and buying puts. You could say they are the mirror image of each other (although the strategies are different).

PART FOUR

HOW TO
BUY PUTS

13

How to Choose Profitable Puts

If you believe the market or your stock is going to drop in value, you have three choices. First, if you are long a stock, you can sell it to avoid future losses. Your second choice is to *sell stocks short*. And your third choice is to *buy puts*. (You can also say you are *long puts*.)

When you buy puts, you profit when the underlying stock goes down in price. For example, in 2006, many housing stocks, which had been doubling and tripling in price for three years, showed signs of weakness. Instead of selling the housing stocks short, you could have bought puts. As the housing stocks fell in price, your puts became more valuable.

Sometimes you get the feeling that put buyers get no respect. Maybe it's because most investors have been programmed to go long. Generally, the public has shied away from shorting strategies. After all, shorting means that you are thinking negatively about stocks. Or perhaps it's because so few people understand how and why you would short stocks.

Note: If you haven't learned how to short stocks, you can read the sidebar at the end of this chapter. It gives a brief but detailed explanation of this fascinating strategy.

In the opinion of many, if you are taking only one side of the market, the long side, you are cutting yourself out of a very lucrative share of the market. When stocks are flat, you can sell covered calls. When stocks are bullish, you can buy calls. And when stocks are bearish, you can buy puts.

In reality, the mechanics of buying puts is the same as buying calls—but in reverse. However, the reason you buy puts is completely different from the reason you buy calls. In fact, if you can understand the reasons why you would buy puts, you will have a huge advantage over many traders, most of whom ignore this extremely useful strategy. It is well worth your time to understand how to buy puts. One day you may need to use this strategy.

What It Means to Buy a Put

When you buy a put, you believe that the underlying stock will decline in price on or before the expiration date. The faster and further the stock declines, the more valuable the put option will be. During a prolonged bear market, when stocks seem to be going down, not up, buying puts could be the only strategy that makes sense.

Because many investors do not feel comfortable shorting stocks, understanding how to buy puts can also give you an edge over other investors. For all of these reasons, it is essential that you learn how to buy puts, even if you don't think you'll ever use this strategy.

Put Power: The Advantages of Buying Puts

Less Risk

Because of margin requirements, you could lose more than you started with when you short stocks, especially if you aren't disciplined. Theoretically, your losses are unlimited (although most short sellers have very strict rules about when to cover their short positions). In addition, when you borrow shares from the brokerage firm, not only are you going on margin but you could be charged an interest rate.

Although it's essential to learn how to short, buying puts can be less risky than selling short. For example, when you buy puts, you can't lose more than your initial investment (margin is not allowed). In addition, when you buy puts, you know in advance how much you can lose. That will help you to control risk.

So if you do use the options market to speculate on stocks going down in value, buying puts can be a lot safer than shorting. And the best part about buying puts is that it's relatively inexpensive.

Unlimited Number of Contracts

Another advantage of buying puts is that you have an unlimited number of options contracts available. As you probably know, when you short stocks, the shares are often not available, especially in a fast-moving or thin market. Therefore, when you buy puts, you usually won't be burdened with special rules that limit when and how you can short the market.

Theoretically, there are an unlimited amount of options contracts, but keep in mind the number of available contracts varies, depending on the popularity of the underlying stock.

Insurance

One of the most effective ways of using puts is to buy them as an insurance policy—to protect your portfolio from disaster (which is why some call it disaster insurance). Ironically, the options exchange was originally designed as "stock insurance" and not for speculation. If you believe that your portfolio or an individual stock is at risk, you can buy puts to cover that period of time. For example, many people were exposed to the Internet stocks during the late 1990s. Had they bought puts during this time to protect their portfolio from crashes or other unforeseen events, their portfolio could have been saved.

Tax Protection

Another use of the options market is for tax management. Perhaps you are worried about the short-term prospects of the market, but for tax reasons you don't want to sell your stocks. So by buying puts, you can leave your stocks intact while protecting them in case of a disaster. Be sure to consult a tax attorney before buying puts for tax management.

An Unsuccessful Google Put

Buying puts can also limit risk as you'll see in this "worst-case" example. (In this case, you'll see that buying puts is less risky than shorting when a stock doesn't work out as you planned.) For example, let's say you wanted to short Google. When Google hit $300 a share, many people thought there was nowhere for it to go but down. If you had shorted this stock, even 100 shares, it would have cost you $30,000.

As it turned out, Google didn't go down but continued to go up to over $400 a share. If you had shorted Google and didn't get out in time, you would be looking at a huge loss, perhaps $10,000 or more (although you should have covered well before then). Nevertheless, for every 1 point that Google went up, you'd have lost $100. Theoretically, you could have had unlimited losses.

On the other hand, if you had bought a put on Google, it might have cost you approximately $10 per contract for a total cost of $1,000. The higher price of the put reflects the higher implied volatility of this stock. It indicates that other traders believe that Google could make extreme moves in either direction.

Nevertheless, one Google put would cost you no more than $1,000, but you'd be in control of $30,000 in stock. The most you could lose on this put would be $1,000. If you were right and Google fell by dozens of points, you could have made huge profits. As it turned out, the stock went up, not down. Instead of a loss of $10,000 or more by shorting, the most you would have lost is $1,000.

Therefore, when a stock doesn't perform as you expected, buying puts makes a lot more sense than shorting. Nevertheless, the best time to use a put option is when you expect an immediate decline in the underlying stock or to protect your long position. But if you are wrong about a stock, a relatively small, limited loss is preferable to potentially unlimited losses.

Selecting the Ideal Market Environment and Underlying Stock

If you are looking for the ideal market environment to buy puts, then you have to think like a short seller. In other words, the more bearish the market environment, the better it is for buying puts. The market often goes down faster than it goes up. It could take weeks or months for the market to build itself up, and in a single day lose all its gains in one dramatic plunge. This happens more often than you think.

The ideal underlying stocks for buying puts are those that are about to fall fast. To find these stocks, you have to use a combination of technical and fundamental analysis. Underlying stocks that have dropped below the 50-day moving average are often good candidates for selling short.

Stocks drop because of a number of factors, but often breaking news will send a stock plummeting. If you can predict in advance when these heart-stopping plunges will occur, you can do very well buying puts. This is easier said than done, as the news on plunging stocks often comes out of nowhere.

A Successful Google Put

Although Google is considered an excellent company with great products, it was unexpectedly hit with bad news. (I apologize for picking on them again.) On February 28, 2006, as reported by the Associated Press: "Google tumbled $28.56 to $361.82 after the Chief Financial Officer told investors that growth at the online search leader was slowing. The CFO told investors at a conference that the company would have to find new ways to boost revenues." As you see, it doesn't take much for investors to brutally punish a stock, at least for a day.

Figure 13-1 is a screen display of the Google puts later that afternoon.

Had you been fortunate enough to have held puts on this stock when the bad news hit that morning, you could have made 200 percent

List	Google Options				Update News	Edit	Delete	Create		
✔	Entry	Trade	Symbol	Last	! ♦	Change	%Change	Bid	Ask	Bid Size	Ask Size
□	1	Trade	GOOG	$363.15	↑	-27.225	-6.97	$363.08	$363.24	3	?
□	2	Trade	GGDON	$18.30	↑	12.70	226.79	$18.10	$18.40	95	171
□	3	Trade	GOPOP	$24.50	↑	15.90	184.88	$24.30	$24.70	29	90
□	4	Trade	GOPOR	$31.83	↓	19.23	152.62	$31.60	$31.90	25	41
□	5	Trade	GGDOL	$13.40	↑	9.70	262.16	$13.10	$13.40	84	219

Figure 13-1   Option Chain: Google Puts

returns on your position within minutes. Notice that although the stock fell by only 7 percent, some of the put options quadrupled.

If you are buying puts for speculation, first look at the overall market environment. The more bearish the market, the better it is for you. Even stocks in good companies go down in a bear market or because of breaking news. Look for stocks that have risen too far and too fast. It doesn't take much for investors' moods to change from greed to fear. Once fear floods the market, investors will head for the exits. That's when you'll be glad you learned how to buy puts.

Note: Remember the first strategy you learned: selling covered calls? Although you would have received a nice premium if you had sold covered calls on Google, you'd have lost money when the underlying stock fell. That is the main reason why volatile technology stocks like Google should be avoided if you are selling covered calls.

Understanding Puts

To buy puts, you have to do your calculations in reverse. After all, you make money when the underlying stock goes down, not up. Therefore, the ideal strike prices will be the exact opposite of those when you're buying calls.

The chart below should help you understand whether a put option is in-the-money, out-of-the-money, or at-the-money:

Is it Out-of-the-Money, At-the-Money, or In-the-Money?

Assume that the underlying stock is currently trading at $30 a share.

Strike Price	Put Option
$40	Deep in-the-money
$35	In-the-money
$30	At-the-money
$25	Out-of-the-money
$20	Far out-of-the-money

To make sense of this chart, you have to think like a short seller. Therefore, the lower the stock goes **below** the strike price, the more valuable the put option (the put option is in-the-money). And, the higher the stock goes **above** the strike price, the less valuable the put option (the put option is out-of-the-money). At first, it might take a while to think in reverse, but once you do, you'll never forget that buying puts is the opposite of buying calls.

How Much Does It Cost?

You calculate the cost of a put the same way you calculate a call. In other words, a $1 option contract will cost you $100. (You are using a multiplier of 100.) To help refresh your memory, let's turn on our calculator. Using the option chain in Figure 13-2, we will buy the April 75 put.

Turn Calculator On   How Much Does a Put Cost?

$3.20 per contract (April 75 put)
× 100 shares of Boeing stock

Total: $320 cost

Explanation: Because the ask price is $3.20 a contract, and a contract equals 100 shares of stock, then the price you pay for buying this option will be $320. If you bought 2 contracts, you would pay $640. If you bought 5 contracts, you would pay $1,600. If you bought 10 contracts, you would pay $3,200. Remember: If you had instead shorted 1,000 shares of the stock, it would have cost you $72,000 plus interest.

How to Calculate Breakeven

The key to your success as an options trader is the ability to calculate risk-reward, and knowing your breakeven point is an important part of this process.

To calculate breakeven for buying puts, let's take a look at our formula.

The put strike price – the contract price = breakeven
$75   – $3.20   = $71.80

Let's see how it looks on our calculator:

Turn Calculator On   Calculating Breakeven

  $75 strike price
– 3.20 contract price

Total: $71.80 breakeven

Explanation: In this example, the underlying stock, Boeing, has to drop to $71.80 a share for you to reach breakeven. Anything below $71.80 is profit. If the stock falls low enough below the strike price, the option could follow the exact movement of the underlying stock. They will trade in unison. By the time the underlying stock has reached this point, the stock is well below the strike price (and the put option is deep in-the-money, as the pros like to say).

The Factors That Influence Puts

The same factors that influenced the call also influence the put: for example, the strike price, the expiration date, the price of the underlying stock, volatility, dividends, and interest rates.

To help you understand the put option more clearly, I'll pull up the Boeing option chain in Figure 13-2. Only put options are displayed.

Strike Prices

Most professional traders would probably suggest that you buy in-the-money puts because they have intrinsic value when you buy. In other

BA		BOEING CO					
Last	**72.69**	↓	-1.44	Bid	**72.51**	Size	**1**
						Puts	
Trade	Symbol	Date · Strike	Last	Change	Bid	Ask	Open Int
Trade	-BAON	Mar 18 06 70.00	$0.35	$0.15	$0.25	$0.35	2561
Trade	-BAOV	Mar 18 06 72.50	$1.05	$0.45	$1.00	$1.10	303
Trade	-BAOO	Mar 18 06 75.00	$2.64	$1.04	$2.50	$2.65	1709
Trade	-BAPN	Apr 22 06 70.00	$1.00	$0.40	$0.85	$0.95	675
Trade	-BAPV	Apr 22 06 72.50	$1.75	$0.65	$1.75	$1.85	481
Trade	-BAPO	Apr 22 06 75.00	$3.10	$0.90	$3.10	$3.20	380
Trade	-BAQL	May 20 06 60.00	$0.20	$0.05	$0.15	$0.20	1542

Figure 13-2   Option Chain: Boeing Puts
Source: Fidelity Investments. Copyright 2002 FMR Corp. All rights reserved.

words, an in-the-money put is worth something. And because you have bought in-the-money puts, you have allowed the stock some room to fall.

For example, in Figure 13-2, the March 75 put is in-the-money by over 2 points. At a cost of $2.65 per contract, it seems pretty reasonable, at least to me. Notice that the April 75 put is only $0.55 more. For only $0.55 more, you gain another month.

Note: It's probably not a brilliant strategy to buy expensive deep in-the-money puts because they are so costly. After all, the whole idea of options is to use less money. Perhaps you should aim for in-the-money puts (one strike price away), which gives you some intrinsic value as well as a relatively reasonable price.

On the other hand, if you buy the cheaper out-of-the-money puts, you would be buying all time value. For example, the April 70 is almost 3 points out-of-the-money, but Boeing would have to drop well below $70 a share for you to make a profit. Nevertheless, out-of-the-money puts give you a greater return if the underlying stock plummets. All of these factors need to be considered when you are buying options.

Here is something to think about. If you are buying puts for the first time, you can start by buying in-the-money puts, but experiment to determine which puts are most profitable.

Expiration Dates

Although you might consider buying puts with one or two months to expiration, you have to find out for yourself which works best for you. Obviously, the longer the time before the option expires, the more expensive it will be. If you choose an option with a month or less to expiration, although cheap, it might not give you enough time for the strategy to play out. Therefore, to balance a reasonable time period and cost, you might think about options with at least a month or more to expiration.

In the example above, the difference between the March 75 put and the April 75 put is a minuscule $0.55. For an extra month, the $0.55 seems like a bargain. In this case, you are paying the extra money for additional time value. The more time you have, the more likely the stock will move as you planned. Therefore, many traders would consider it a bargain to pay only $.55 for an extra month of time.

What Is a Profitable Put?

After talking to professional traders as well as relying on my own personal experience and extensive research, the profile of a profitable put is clear (although there are exceptions). And the winner is....

. . . .

A profitable put = A relatively low premium with a strike price and expiration date that gives you the highest reward with the least risk.

. . . .

It's true that out-of-the-money puts offer bigger profits for a cheaper price. But the risk that the underlying stock will drop far enough to be profitable is a long shot. Yes, miracles do happen, but you are trading not based on miracles or luck but on skill and probabilities.

Important: One of the biggest advantages of choosing an in-the-money put is that a moderate move in the underlying stock can still bring you profits.

Caveat: Once again, keep in mind the above profile is only a starting point. There are always exceptions to what I consider a profitable put. To be on the safe side, you should practice trading options by buying only 1 put contract at a time. This will give you a good idea of how you can profit from falling stocks. By all means, experiment with various strike prices and expiration dates. As I said before, your long-term goal is to devise your own criteria for what is the best put rather than depending on authors or other traders to tell you what and how to trade.

---

*What It Means to Short Stocks**

If you are going to buy put options, it is helpful to understand how to short stocks. Therefore, the following is an overview of this rather fascinating but misunderstood strategy.

When you invest in a stock hoping that it will rise in price, you are said to be *long* the stock. Your goal is to buy low and sell high. Your profit is the difference between the price at which you bought the stock and your selling price.

On the other hand, if you hope that a stock will go down in price, you are said to be *short* the stock. When you short a stock, you first sell the stock, hoping to buy it back at a lower price. Your profit is the difference between the price at which you sold the stock and the price at which you bought it back. If you've never shorted stocks, it sounds strange until you do it a few times.

Imagine making money when a stock goes down in price? For many people, it sounds unethical to profit from a falling stock. In reality, you're in the market for only one reason: to make money. It doesn't matter whether you go long or short as long as you make profits. It's neither unethical nor inappropriate to short stocks. It's a sophisticated strategy that allows you to profit even during dismal economic conditions.

For example, let's say you are watching the stock Tracking, Inc., and you believe that over the next month it will go down in price. Perhaps there is negative news about the industry, or perhaps you notice that the company has a lot of debt. You decide to short 100 shares of Tracking, Inc., at the current market price of $20 a share, so you call your brokerage firm or use your online account. When you place the order, the brokerage firm will lend you 100 shares of Tracking, Inc. (because you don't own it). Let's say Tracking, Inc., falls to $18 a share. You now buy back the shares that you borrowed for a 2-point profit.

In the past, you could only short when a stock is temporarily rising, called the "uptick rule." In 2006, this controversial rule was removed, allowing short sellers to short stocks at anytime, even if the stock is plunging. A more important rule: You can't short a stock whose price is less than $5 a share.

Although selling short sounds like a straightforward strategy, a lot of things can go wrong. First, when you go long a stock, the most you can lose is everything you invested. (I know. That can still be pretty bad.) On the other hand, when you short a stock, you can lose more than you invested, which is why shorting can be risky. Let's see how this works.

If you sell short 100 shares of Tracking, Inc., at $20 a share, you receive $2,000. If Tracking, Inc., drops to $18 a share, you made 2 points, or a $200 profit. Let's say you are wrong and Tracking, Inc., goes higher. For every point Tracking, Inc., goes up, you lose $100. How high can Tracking, Inc., rise? The answer is frightening:

an infinite amount! The problem with shorting is that if the stock goes up, not down, your losses are incalculable.

I knew a group of investors who shorted Yahoo! in 1997 when it reached $90 a share. They were convinced that Yahoo! was overpriced. Perhaps they were technically correct, but that didn't stop the stock from soaring to as high as $400 one year later. In 1999, it actually went over $1,000 a share for a *split-adjusted* price of $445.

These investors were forced to buy back the shares early, losing over 100 points, because the losses grew so large. A few years later, after the market came to its senses, Yahoo! dropped to less than $20 a share (adjusted for splits), but it was too late for my acquaintances. Keep in mind that most experienced short sellers are disciplined enough to cover their short position before a stock goes against them that much.

One rule about shorting that fits in nicely with buying puts: It's called *shorting* for a reason. You don't want to short for very long. Stocks tend to go up more than they go down, so holding a short position for too long can be risky. Also, by being short, you could be paying margin interest, and, as you know, shorting stocks can be risky if you don't use stops. You must closely monitor any and all short positions.

---

*Some of the text used in this sidebar originally appeared in my previous book *Understanding Stocks* (McGraw-Hill, 2003).

· ·

Now that you've learned how to choose profitable puts, you will next learn how to manage your put position.

14

Managing Your Put Position

In this chapter, I'll discuss the risks and management of your put position. Since you've already learned how to buy calls, this chapter should be relatively easy. After all, managing a put position is similar to managing a call position. The hard part, as usual, is exiting the position with profits. Once again, that is why it's essential that you have a trading plan. Before I discuss the trading plan, however, I'd like to review some of the risks of using this strategy.

What to Expect from Buying Puts

Figure 14-1 is a visual representation of the risks and rewards of buying puts. The advantage of buying puts is that, unlike shorting stocks, your profit potential is substantial whereas your losses are limited. Only you can decide if this strategy makes sense for you and for what you are trying to achieve.

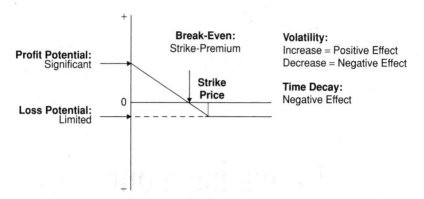

Figure 14-1   Risks and Rewards of Buying Puts
Source: CBOE Copyright 2006 All rights reserved.

The Risks of Buying Puts

As I said before, the risks of buying puts are actually similar to buying calls. As you know, it's estimated that most options contracts held to expiration expire unexercised, although the exact percentage is hard to determine. And it's well accepted that many speculators lose money trading options. So if your only reason for buying puts is for speculation, then the odds are against your making a profit, although it's still possible to do well. (As it turned out, buying puts on many of the housing stocks in early 2006 was exactly the right move.)

In addition, if you are using put options to protect your portfolio or to occasionally speculate, then you are on the right track—assuming you take steps to limit risk.

The biggest risk in buying puts, just as with buying calls, is that you could lose your entire investment. Although buying puts is usually cheaper than shorting and you won't lose more than you invested, there is still a chance your option will expire worthless by expiration. Your risk is limited when you buy puts, but you can still lose 100 percent of your investment.

Perhaps knowing that the odds are against you could motivate you to work harder to be successful. This means doing more intensive research, studying more, and becoming a more disciplined trader.

Unfortunately, many people get too emotional when trading. For example, even after making a huge gain, many traders don't sell.

For some reason, they believe the profits will continue to multiply and are unwilling to appreciate that profits, like options, are fleeting. Put options are even more fleeting because markets tend to go up more than they go down. So if you do make money by buying puts, you should cash in your profits according to your trading plan (which usually means as quickly as possible).

Buying puts is difficult because you have to be correct on the direction as well as on the timing of the underlying stock. More often than not, an option ends up close to where it started, and you can lose your entire investment (if you don't sell, that is). Buying puts, like buying calls, is not an easy strategy, but it's very effective in down markets.

Buying Puts: Step-by-Step

The good news is that it's easy to buy puts (it's similar to buying calls). The only difference between buying calls and puts is the option symbol. For example, let's say you wanted to buy the Boeing April 75 put, BAPO, as shown in Figure 14-2.

Step One: After entering the correct account and option symbol, you check the ask price. In this example, the ask price is $3.20. This option is in-the-money by 2 points.

Step Two: You choose Buy to Open and enter a limit price of $3.20 good for the day only. In options terminology, you opened a position to buy a put. See Figure 14-3.

	BA	BOEING CO						
Last	72.69	↓	-1.44	Bid	72.51	Size		1
						Puts		
Trade	Symbol	Date - Strike	Last	Change	Bid	Ask	Open Int
Trade	-BAON	Mar 18 06 70.00	$0.35	$0.15	$0.25	$0.35	2561
Trade	-BAOV	Mar 18 06 72.50	$1.05	$0.45	$1.00	$1.10	303
Trade	-BAOO	Mar 18 06 75.00	$2.64	$1.04	$2.50	$2.65	1709
Trade	-BAPN	Apr 22 06 70.00	$1.00	$0.40	$0.85	$0.95	675
Trade	-BAPV	Apr 22 06 72.50	$1.75	$0.65	$1.75	$1.85	481
Trade	-BAPO	Apr 22 06 75.00	$3.10	$0.90	$3.10	$3.20	380
Trade	-BAQL	May 20 06 60.00	$0.20	$0.05	$0.15	$0.20	1542

Figure 14-2   Option Chain: Boeing Puts
Source: Fidelity Investments. Copyright 2002 FMR Corp. All rights reserved.

Symbol	Last	Chg.	Bid	Ask	Action	Qty	Order Type	Price	Trail Amt.	TIF
-BAPO ▼	3.25	0.15	3.10	3.30	▼	1 ÷	Limit ▼	$3.20 ÷	÷	Day ▼

Figure 14-3   Put Order Entry Screen
Source: Fidelity Investments. Copyright 2002 FMR Corp. All rights reserved

> *Step Three*: Before you place the order, it's recommended that
> you preview the order. This will prevent any unnecessary
> and costly mistakes.
> *Step Four*: Press the enter key and send in the order. Your
> account will be debited by the full amount.

Broker Instructions: If you called your broker and wanted to place the
above order by phone, you would say, "I want to buy one put for Boeing April 75 for a limit price of $3.20 (or better) good for the day only.

Note: If you do decide to place a call with a broker, the recorded telephone call is a valid contract. Be sure to speak clearly and use options
terminology to place the trade.

Your Trading Plan

If there is anything you've learned in this book, it's that buying an option
is the easiest part of trading. The hard work begins as soon as you press
the enter key and send in the order. To plan for any outcome, it's essential you think of what you would do before you place your order.

As you know, when you buy puts, the underlying stock can only
move in three directions: up, down, or sideways. Let's analyze how
you would react under each scenario. To refresh your memory, we had
previously bought the Boeing April 75 put, BAPO, for the ask price of
$3.20 (don't be surprised when it changes).

Note: You must keep a close eye on both the underlying stock and
option if you want to make a profitable trade. The underlying stock
will help determine the direction of the put. Remember that wherever
the underlying stock goes, your option will probably follow (although
there are exceptions).

The Underlying Stock Moves Up

Outcome: The stock moves above the strike price.

What to expect: This is not what you wanted. (Remember, these are puts, not calls.) As the underlying stock moves up, the put option will deteriorate in value. As the stock moves higher than the strike price, the option will drop in value and eventually become worthless.

Analysis: If the put goes in the wrong direction, you can either sell part of your position (assuming you bought more than one put), hoping to salvage something. You can also hold on longer, hoping that the stock will eventually drop in value. If you do decide to hold on, you have to weigh many factors, including how much time is left until expiration, volatility, and whether there is a chance the stock will reverse direction.

When you are wrong, as a put buyer, the most you can lose is your entire investment. If you were shorting, your losses could be unlimited (if you didn't cover the position, that is).

Nevertheless, managing an option when it goes against you requires skill and discipline. This is what separates the pros from the novices. It's hard enough to manage your winners, but it takes a tremendous amount of skill to manage losers.

The Underlying Stock Stays the Same

Outcome: The stock stays at or near the same strike price.

What to expect: This is not an ideal situation. If the underlying stock is stuck in neutral, the option will lose value, especially as it gets closer to the expiration date.

Analysis: Because there is still some intrinsic value left in the option, you can either sell for a partial gain or wait a bit longer, hoping for a turnaround. As you know, hope is not a practical investment strategy.

If you do wait, you will also lose time value, especially as the stock gets closer to the expiration date. Only you can decide whether to cut your losses and sell, or wait for a miracle to save your position.

The Underlying Stock Moves Down

Outcome: The stock falls, dropping *below* the strike price. Remember, these are puts.

What to expect: As a put buyer, this is exactly what you want and expect. The longer and lower the underlying stock falls below the strike price, the more valuable the option could become.

Analysis: As the underlying stock falls, the price of the put option moves up. If the stock falls far enough, you can wait until expiration, trying to squeeze out the last bit of profit. When you buy put options, it makes sense to take profits quickly, as stocks sometimes rebound rapidly.

If your stock is below the strike price, your other choice is to sell the put on or before the expiration date and book the profits. You select Sell to Close, just as you did when you bought calls. You have another choice, however, and that is to exercise the put.

What It Means to Exercise a Put Option

When you were a call buyer, you had the right to exercise the option and buy the underlying stock. As a put buyer, you also have the right to exercise the option. But exercising a put option is different than exercising a call option. In fact, exercising a put will seem a little strange at first. Why? When you exercise a put option, it means you are exchanging your profitable put option and converting it into a short position. In other words, after you exercise the put, you are now shorting (or selling) shares of the underlying stock. (At first, this may seem confusing.)

In other words, you have the right to short (or sell) the underlying stock on or before the expiration date. You are not required to exercise the option and short the stock, but you can if you wish. Put another way (no pun intended), if you decide to exercise the put, then you will suddenly be the proud owner of a short position.

The main reason you would exercise a put option is that you believe the stock will keep going *down*. By exercising, you can continue to profit if the stock price moves lower. Do you remember at what price you exercise the option? The answer: at the strike price. In other words, you have the right to exercise the option and short the stock at the strike price.

For example, let's say that IBM is currently trading at $80 a share. You decide to exercise 1 put at the 85 strike price. As soon as you exercise, your put is converted to a short position. You are now short 100 shares of IBM at $85 a share. (Since IBM is trading at $80 a share, after exercising the option at the 85 strike price, you will already have a five-point profit.)

Hint: Keep in mind that although you have the right to exercise a put, most put buyers prefer to sell the option rather than convert to a short position.

To Exercise Your Put Option

The procedure for exercising a put option is the same as for exercising a call option. To repeat, you *must* first notify your brokerage firm (preferably by phone) that you plan to exercise your option. You should let them know at least 24 hours before the brokerage firm's cutoff time on Expiration Friday. If your option is in-the-money and you don't notify the brokerage firm of your decision, your option could expire unused. This could cause complications to your account.

Many put buyers wait until the expiration date to exercise their option, but American-style options can technically be exercised at anytime. Once the option is exercised, however, the exercise is irrevocable.

As the put buyer, when you exercise a put, you usually have no stock shares to deliver to the put seller. Because you have no stock to deliver, you must short the stock. This short position appears the next day and settles in three business days.

Advanced Put Strategies

The Protective Put: A Form of Stock Insurance

The put strategies I have previously discussed are primarily for speculators who want to make profits from a falling stock. The advantage of buying puts is that you will participate in the losing stock without actually having to short it.

There is, however, another very clever use of the put. If you buy a put on a stock that you own to protect it from danger, you are said to be buying a *protective put*. If you buy a protective put, you are protecting a long stock position you already own. It's like an insurance policy for your stocks.

Buying protective puts makes sense if you have reason to believe the stock is due for a nasty fall. This helps you to limit your downside risk. This strategy would have made sense in the late 1990s or early 2000 if you had owned an Internet stock. Perhaps you had reason to believe that the Internet stocks were overvalued (and many were) and wanted to protect your portfolio. You use a protective put when you are concerned with the downside and you want to protect the underlying security. The price you pay is similar to an insurance premium.

Some people don't want to sell their stocks for tax purposes, even if they think the stocks might fall in price. If you buy a protective put, you can hold your long positions and still have protection in case your stocks drop in value.

Often, people who buy protective puts will buy an amount of puts that equal the number of shares they have in their account. For example, if you own 1,000 shares of GE and believe it might go down in the short term, you buy 10 put contracts. If you are right and GE goes down, then the value of the put will rise (as long as it's in-the-money), keeping your portfolio balanced. (Nevertheless, you shouldn't rely on puts to fully protect you from worst-case scenarios).

Although buying protective puts sound like a wise idea, you also don't want to throw your money away. If you are so concerned your stock might plunge, perhaps you should think of selling your stock rather than paying for protection.

Advanced Hint: If you are *shorting* stocks, you can also buy *call* options as protection for your short position.

The Married Put

The term *married put* comes from an old IRS ruling. The term has lingered for years even though it's no longer recognized by the IRS. The strategy refers to simultaneously buying the underlying stock and the put option. Similar to the protective put, it's a hedging strategy designed to protect the underlying stock. The difference is that with a protective put, you buy the put *after* you buy the stock. With the married put, you buy the put at the same time.

For example, you enter an order to buy 100 shares of Tracking, Inc., and simultaneously buy 1 put on Tracking, Inc. If you bought 500 shares of Tracking, Inc., you'd buy 5 puts. The put is acting as an insurance policy against any possible downturns or sudden drops in the stock. If the stock doesn't plunge, then all you lost was what you paid for the option. On the other hand, if the stock does take a dive, then the put will protect you from disaster.

Hint: Once again, if you are so nervous about the prospects of a stock that you have to buy a put to protect your position, perhaps you shouldn't buy the stock in the first place.

The Collar: Protecting Your Covered Call

As you know, one of the downsides to selling covered calls is that the underlying stock could fall in price. There is a strategy called a *collar* or *protective collar* that can protect the underlying stock when selling covered calls.

If, after selling a covered call, you believe the underlying stock will tumble, you can initiate a collar. Perhaps the stock has had a nice upward run but you want to protect your gains. By initiating a collar, you are reducing your risk in return for less upside opportunity. The pros say you are buying downside protection.

Here's one example of how the collar works:

1. You sold a covered call for Tracking, Inc., for the June 55 strike price, for which you received $1.90 in premium, or $190. Tracking, Inc., is currently trading at $49.25 so it has a lot of room to move up.
2. You *buy* an out-of-the-money June 47.5 put for a cost of $0.90 each for a total of $90. The put is your collar, protecting your covered call. Think of the $90 as an insurance premium for protecting the underlying stock.
3. If Tracking, Inc., goes up in price or stays the same, the put option expires worthless. You lost $90 for the unused insurance.

4. On the other hand, if Tracking, Inc., drops in price, the put option will become more valuable.

5. You have to decide whether to hold or sell the put or hold or sell the underlying stock. Most important, the put you bought acts like a protective collar around your covered call.

Risks: Although on paper this strategy sounds wonderful, if the underlying stock does fall, you might not gain as much on the put as you lost on the stock. Once again, don't completely depend on the collar to save your portfolio if the underlying stock plunges.

Note: If you're comfortable with the underlying stock, perhaps you won't need to buy a put to protect your covered call.

The Relationship between Stocks and Options

After you have placed your option order, it's essential that you closely monitor the underlying stock as well as the option. In fact, one of the most fascinating aspects of options is studying the relationship between the stock and the option. Many books have been written on this important relationship, and there are many complicated formulas to help professional traders understand it. You could spend months studying how the two securities relate to each other. As you know, however, you are particularly concerned with the underlying stock.

There is one observation you can make right away. On a pure *percentage* basis, it is not uncommon to see the underlying stock move up or down 1 percent while the option moves 25 percent or more. In Figure 14-4, Google made a relatively small move of 2.63 percent while the call options made big percentage moves.

List	Google Options			▾ Update News	Edit Delete Create				
✔	Entry	Trade	Symbol	Last	! ⬍	Change	%Change	Bid	Ask	Bid Size
☐	1	Trade	**GOOG**	$387.31	⬇	9.91	2.63	$387.30	$387.42	1
☐	2	Trade	**-GGDCJ**	$41.30	⬇	8.80	27.09	$40.80	$41.30	61
☐	3	Trade	**-GGDCD**	$69.40		10.20	17.23	$68.80	$69.30	58

Figure 14-4   The Relationship between Stocks and Options: Google
Source: Fidelity Investments. Copyright 2002 FMR Corp. All rights reserved.

✔	Entry	Trade	Symbol	Last	!♦	Change	%Change	Bid	Ask	Bid Size	Ask Size
List Apollo					▾ Update News	Edit Delete Create					
⌐	1	Trade	APOL	$49.33	▼	-9.14	-15.63	$49.32	$49.35	5	5 1
⌐	2	Trade	-OAQOK	$5.60	↑	5.30	1,766.67	$5.60	$5.80	130	94
⌐	3	Trade	-OAQOL	$10.20	↑	8.00	363.64	$10.60	$10.80	39	85
⌐	4	Trade	OAQOM	$15.60	↑	8.60	122.86	$15.60	$15.80	39	85

Figure 14-5   The Relationship between Stocks and Options: Apollo
Source: Fidelity Investments. Copyright 2002 FMR Corp. All rights reserved.

Advanced Note: If you are an experienced trader, you will use delta to calculate how much the option is "theoretically" expected to increase or decrease. (Delta is explained in Chapter 15.)

Sometimes the options can make extreme moves, as in Figure 14-5. The stock, Apollo (Nasdaq: APOL), fell by only 15 percent, but the put option increased by almost 2,000 percent.

Although at first glance it looks like the option outperforms the stock, it is actually quite misleading. Obviously, if you look at percentages only, a few pennies' move in the stock can cause the option to appear to move much higher. In fact, some people will compare the percentage move to make you believe that buying calls or puts will give you far greater returns than buying stocks. To do an accurate comparison, however, you need to compare the shares of the two securities, not how much the option moves up or down on a percentage basis. Again, the pros will use delta to make an accurate comparison.

Let's take a closer look at the relationship between the underlying stock and option. In Figure 14-4, it would cost you approximately $38,000 to buy 100 shares of Google. If (and this is a big if) you had taken that $38,000 and bought the call option, GGDCJ, you would have made an amazing 27 percent return. But taking such a large position in one option is incredibly risky, even foolish, unless you are a professional. Therefore, it's unfair and misleading to compare the stock and option dollar by dollar.

What is fair is to compare shares and contracts. The 100 shares you bought in Google is equal to one call contract. Instead of paying $38,000 for 100 shares of Google, you paid $413 ($41.30 × 100). Therefore, you made 27 percent on the $413 you paid for the contract. Although you can make extraordinary returns in the options market, it's risky to invest the same amount of dollars in an option as you would a stock.

While I'm on the subject, many people think the options market is separate from the stock market. In fact, the two markets are linked, like a horse and cart. The stock market is in front, like the horse. The options market follows behind.

Although options do influence the stock market at times (it's estimated that 10 percent of stock trades are influenced by calls and puts being bought, sold, and exercised), this is the exception, not the rule. Normally, however, the underlying stock leads, and the option follows.

===================================

· ·

Now that you know how to buy puts, you're going to learn more advanced options strategies. As usual, you might want to take a break before moving to Part Five. You will soon be entering the world of the experienced options trader.

PART FIVE

ADVANCED OPTIONS STRATEGIES

15

Straddles and Spreads

Some of you have been waiting a long time to learn about the more advanced strategies. Perhaps you took an expensive seminar or class and need a quick review. Or perhaps you are planning on taking a class and want to know what to expect. Nevertheless, the advanced strategies included in Part Five are the playground of the pros. There is no doubt that many of these strategies are quite intriguing and flexible.

Although this is technically an introductory book, you should learn everything you can about advanced strategies. One way to improve as a trader is to experiment with all the strategies, as long as you don't trade with more than one contract at a time. There is no rush with this learning process. You can easily spend a year mastering Level 1 and Level 2 options strategies before you even attempt the strategies included in this section.

If you are truly interested in entering the realm of professional trading, this is a good place to start. And even if you have little interest in advanced strategies, it makes sense to understand these strategies in case you have to use them one day.

In addition, your ultimate goal is to gain an edge over other traders. By learning all of the strategies in this book, you will be one step closer to that goal.

Caveat: This section is only meant to be an introduction to advanced options strategies. To find out more about these strategies, read the recommended list of intermediate and professional books in Chapter 18.

Double the Trouble

In this chapter, you will be introduced to two options strategies: *straddles* and *spreads* (often referred to as Level 3 options strategies). If you thought it was hard to buy and sell calls and puts, how about buying and selling both at the same time? That, in a nutshell, is the idea of straddles and spreads. Keep in mind that the more complex some of these strategies get, the higher the risk. (Some traders will disagree. Nevertheless, the more complex the trade, the more difficult it is to unwind.)

Straddles: Searching for Profits

The official definition of a *straddle* from the Options Industry Council (OIC): "A trading position involving puts and calls on a one-to-one basis in which the puts and calls have the same strike price, expiration, and underlying stock."

The definition of a *long straddle* from Investopedia.com: "An options strategy with which the investor holds a position in both a call and put with the same strike price and expiration date."

In other words, this strategy involves buying both a call and a put with the same underlying stock, strike price, and expiration date. You make a profit if the underlying stock moves in one direction or the other. You could say this is the strategy for those who can't make up their mind and want to cover both the bull and bear position.

For example, if you buy the Home Depot January 40 *call* and the Home Depot January 40 *put*, you have initiated a straddle. Therefore, if the underlying stock makes a huge move in either direction, you could make a profit. Either the call will be profitable and the put expires worthless (or you sell it for a loss), or the put will be profitable and the call expires worthless (or you sell it for a loss).

The way you lose on both sides of the straddle is if the stock doesn't move at all or not enough to cover *both* premiums. For example, if Home Depot remains at or near $40 a share by the expiration date, both the call and the put will expire worthless. Unfortunately, that happens more often than you think.

• •

Important Definition: Each side of the straddle is called a leg. So in the above example, you would say that one leg of the option will be profitable while the other leg will not.

• •

For a long straddle to be profitable, you're looking for a stock that will explode in one direction or the other. This could be a volatile stock that will rise or fall quickly before the expiration date. Before you think of super-volatile stocks, remember that you also don't want to pay too much for the option. If you choose an underlying stock that is too volatile, the cost will be so high it will be hard for you to make a profit.

In the real world, the underlying stock often makes a move in one direction, but before you can close the position and make a profit, the stock reverses direction. Then you end up where you started, losing money on both legs (both sides of the straddle position). Occasionally, there's not enough liquidity to quickly close down both legs, which complicates your trading life (although it sounds so easy in the classroom).

Nevertheless, there are times when a straddle makes sense. For example, let's say the Fed is going to announce whether it will raise interest rates. You are convinced the market is going to react strongly to the news, and move violently in one direction or the other. Unfortunately, you can't predict which direction. By buying a straddle, or two contracts that are the opposite of each other, you have both sides covered.

In the case of the Fed announcement, you could buy a straddle on an index or a financial institution like a bank. Perhaps the option price will be low enough so that the losing leg won't be a huge loss. Whether interest rates go higher or lower, the stock or index should react.

Advanced Note: The pros like straddles because you can keep the premium on one leg and close the other—what the pros call a directionless strategy. Unlike other options strategies, direction isn't important with straddles. On the other hand, you care a lot about volatility. This strategy works best if an option has high implied volatility and is sure to move in one direction or the other. It's tricky, however, because you never know what an option will ultimately do.

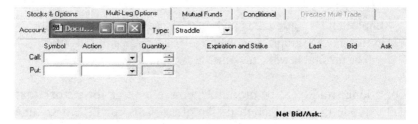

Figure 15-1   Straddle Order Entry Screen
Source: Fidelity Investments. Copyright 2002 FMR Corp. All rights reserved.

The Risks of Trading Straddles

Straddles are a specialized strategy that you probably won't use every day. If the underlying stock goes nowhere, both legs of the contract will expire worthless. The goal is to make your profit as soon as the stock reacts. Otherwise, you could lose money as time expires. It does take a lot of work and calculations to be profitable using this strategy, although there are many stories of beginner's luck.

Figure 15-1 shows an example of a straddle order screen. Notice that you must enter a call and put order simultaneously.

Spreads

If you thought straddles were fun, then you will love spreads. Many people are fascinated by the idea of spreads. There are dozens of sexy sounding but complex spreads: for example, the butterfly spread, the condor spread, the diagonal spread, the vertical spread, the calendar spread, the bull spread, and the bear spread. In fact, there is a spread strategy for nearly everyone, no matter how bullish, bearish, or in between you might be.

If you think that buying a single call or a single put is boring, you can simultaneously trade two, three, or even four options positions. It's easy to be dazzled or confused by these various strategies. By the end of this chapter, however, you should have a better idea about whether spreads fit in with your trading strategy.

Let's start with the official definition of spreads from the OIC: "A position consisting of two parts, each of which alone would profit from opposite directional price moves. As orders, these opposite parts are entered and executed simultaneously in the hope of (1) limiting risk, or (2) benefiting from a change of price relationship between the two parts."

And from Investopedia.com: "An options position established by purchasing one option and selling another option of the same class but of a different series."

In other words, instead of making one transaction you are making two transactions, and usually at the same time. Often, the goal is to use one option position to protect another option position.

Note: Perhaps you've noticed with these strategies that you seem to be more concerned with trading, hedging, and protecting option positions than with the underlying stocks. That is correct. Your strategies are based on the buying and selling of options contracts—not stocks.

Why Buy Spreads?

What is fascinating about spreads is that you are using the money from selling one call to finance the buying of another call. In other words, you are using the premium from selling one leg to pay for the cost of the other leg.

Traders also view spreads as a form of insurance, except instead of protecting your stock position, you are protecting your option position. In some ways, it's like option insurance. Spreads can be as complex as you want to make them, which is why many professional traders are attracted to them.

Two Types of Spreads

There are two types of spreads: the more common *vertical spread*, and the very uncommon *horizontal spread*. (I won't discuss horizontal spread strategies in this book because they are so limited.) An example of a vertical spread is buying a call at one strike price but selling a call at a higher strike price. For example, you could *buy* a call for Home Depot at a 40 strike price but *sell* a call for Home Depot at a 45 strike price. This is a vertical spread because you are buying a call at one strike price and then selling a call at the next strike price up.

For example, the bull call spread strategy is based on the fact that the stock will go up. You will take the revenue you receive from selling the one call to finance the purchase of the other call. By doing this spread, even though you are limiting your gain, you are also controlling any potential loss.

In the last few years some brokerage firms have offered to do some of the preparation and homework, whereby you click on a button and choose spreads from a computer model.

Bull Call Spread

The *bull call spread* is one of the most popular vertical spreads. The official definition from the OIC: "The simultaneous purchase of one call option with a lower strike price and the writing of another call option with a higher strike price."

In a bull call spread, you want the underlying stock to go sideways or up in price. For example, you buy a call at one strike price and sell another call at a higher strike price. Both options have the same expiration date. If the underlying stock moves up in price, and moves up a lot, then you will make a profit.

Ideally, you are looking for an underlying stock that is moving up consistently. Although the premium will be attractive (on the leg you are selling), a stock that is too volatile could unwind very quickly. To exit this spread, you will typically close out both legs simultaneously. The reason the bull call spread is so popular is that you don't have to put up very much money. It costs less than buying a call because you are using the money from one leg to finance the other leg.

For example, you buy an October 30 call while simultaneously selling the October 35 call. An aggressive bull call spread strategy is to select calls that are out-of-the-money. A less aggressive bull call spread is to select calls that are in-the-money. On the other hand, if you select two calls that are in-the-money, you are limiting your profits.

When you do a bull call spread, in a way you are "setting parameters." Rather than simply buying one call, you are making a double bet, which could also increase your gains. If you are right, you could make substantial profits, although that depends on which calls you select. The bigger the risks you take with this strategy, the more money you can make. If you can't sleep at night after initiating a bull call spread, you'd be better off taking less risk and accepting smaller profits. Only you can determine how much risk and reward you are willing to accept.

Bear Call Spread

In the *bear call spread*, you are expecting the underlying stock to stay sideways or go a bit lower. The official definition from the OIC: "The simultaneous purchase of one call option with a higher strike price and the writing of another call option with a lower strike price."

For example, you *buy* a call option that is one strike price and *sell* a call on the same stock at a lower strike price. If the underlying stock actually declines, you will profit, although there is limited profit and limited loss. Once again, if you are that bearish on the underlying stock, you might consider buying a put.

For example, let's say you buy the October 40 call and sell the October 35 call. You are taking in money for selling the 35 and using that money to buy the 40. By using this strategy, you hope that the stock will drop in price and both options will expire worthless. That way, you won't have to pay anything to close the spread. What could go wrong? If the underlying stock moves above the 40 call, then you could lose money, although your loss will be limited. Typically, to exit this spread, you will close out both legs simultaneously.

Butterfly Spread

If you thought that making two transactions simultaneously was enjoyable, then you'll love the butterfly spread, a combination of the bull and bear spread. You'll notice from the following definition that we are entering the realm of the professional trader. From the OIC: "A strategy involving three strike prices that has both limited risk and limited profit potential. A long call butterfly is established by buying one call at the lowest strike price, writing two calls at the middle strike price, and buying one call at the highest strike price. A long put butterfly is established by buying one put at the highest strike price, writing two puts at the middle strike price, and buying one put at the lowest strike price."

In other words, you buy one call at the higher and lower strike price but sell two calls at the middle strike price. This strategy involves limited risk but also limited gains. Instead of two strike prices, you are now looking at three strike prices. Although the name is fascinating, managing three strike prices simultaneously can be complicated. To exit this spread, you will close out all three legs.

Observation: I've noticed that people who want to prove they know a lot about options always say they're doing butterfly spreads. Maybe the pros are, but it takes a lot of experience to simultaneously manage three legs and still be profitable. And although the risk of trading the butterfly spread is limited, you can still lose 100 percent of your investment.

The Problems and Risks of Trading Spreads

If you are just starting to trade options, there is probably nothing wrong with experimenting with spreads as long as you start by trading only one contract at a time. You'll discover that it takes a lot of effort and experience to get the correct price, premium, and expiration date. It also requires an understanding of the underlying stock. Obviously, many professional traders do spreads on a daily basis. They use the revenue they receive from selling one leg of the call to finance buying the other leg.

As you know from reading this book, options can be as simple or as complex as you want to make them. When you add multiple factors like two strike prices and two premiums, many things can go against you.

When you first hear about spreads, they sound wonderful and inexpensive, especially if you see them in a textbook or hear about them in a classroom. Unfortunately, sometimes these positions are difficult to unwind once they are established. In the real world, the underlying stock and option don't often behave as you expected. Sometimes one leg goes in one direction and the other leg in another. As a result, the premiums on these positions change at different times, causing a loss.

It's similar to a juggling act. It's easy to juggle two balls. But when you start juggling three, it's not so easy anymore. And if you are juggling four balls, it takes focus, experience, practice, and skill. When you are trading spreads, it's like juggling four balls. For example, if you complete one leg but not the other leg, you could have a bit of a mess.

In addition, trading spreads is a limited strategy with limited results. You are limited in how much revenue you can receive. It's also difficult because of its complexity.

Also, when you sell calls or puts, you have exposed yourself to a "naked" or *uncovered* position, which will be explained in the next chapter. Although the idea is to close out the legs before you are required to buy the underlying stock, if you make a mistake or don't fully appreciate the risks, you could be looking at substantial losses.

These strategies are based on the movement of the underlying stock (as well as volatility). If you are so good at choosing the correct stock, then perhaps you'd be better off buying a call option (or even investing in the stock). In fact, traders often get so distracted by the complicated options strategies that they forget what underlying stock they are trading.

On the other hand, there are experts who routinely do spreads and other complicated options strategies. If you are truly interested in spreads, first learn the basic options strategies. When you've truly mastered the basics, then you'll be ready to move on to advanced level options strategies.

The Delta Effect

For many people, *delta* sounds like Greek to them, and that's exactly what it is. There are other Greek terms used to describe the relationship between the underlying stock and option, including *theta*, *gamma*, *rho*, and *vega*. The good news is that all of the Greeks can be easily calculated online by simply entering known information about your option. Fortunately, the CBOE and OIC have online software that calculates the delta for you. The software then displays a number which gives you important clues about your option.

Delta, for example, measures how much an option changes when the price of the underlying stock changes. Every change in the stock will cause a change in the delta. In other words, delta indicates how much an option is expected to move for every dollar move in the stock.

Knowing the delta can help you identify the chances that your option will be profitable at expiration. Trading options is all about percentages and probability, which is why so many options traders rely on delta to give them an edge over other traders. Once you realize how helpful delta is when buying options, you might not want to trade without it.

Analyzing Delta

The next part is a little technical but once you understand what the numbers mean, it will seem relatively easy. The delta is displayed as a decimal between 0 and +1 for call options and 0 and −1 for put options. (In this sidebar, we will only be discussing *call* options). For example, if the IBM call option moves up $0.40 while IBM moves up a dollar, it would be a .40 delta (a rate of 40/100). In this case, a .40 delta suggests that the option has a 40 percent probability of being profitable (another way of saying in-the-money) at expiration. If the stock continues to rise, then the delta would also rise, perhaps rising to .45 or .50.

A .25 delta has only a 25 percent probability of being in-the-money at expiration. A .50 delta suggests that an option has a 50 percent probability of being in-the-money at expiration. And finally, a .80 delta suggests that the call option has an 80 percent probability of being in-the-money at expiration. This is obviously very useful information, giving you a rough estimate your option will be profitable.

Therefore, stocks that are well below the strike price (or out-of-the-money calls) tend to have smaller deltas, while stocks that are above the strike price (or in-the-money calls) tend to have larger deltas. That is why when you buy an out-of-the-money call, there is a probability it will expire worthless. Why? The delta is so small that it is harder for the option to move fast enough to become profitable before the expiration date. (By the way, a delta of .80 will be more expensive to buy than a delta of .50 or .30.)

Another Observation: As the call option approaches expiration, its delta will be 1.00. As a put option approaches expiration, on the other hand, its delta will be −1.00. Therefore, a 1.00 delta on a call option is as sweet as it gets. It means that for every point move in the stock, there will be a corresponding point move in the option. For options traders, it doesn't get any better than that.

Delta Reveals the Truth

Many traders want to know how the underlying stock can make a huge move and yet they didn't make any money. In fact, the option didn't budge at all. The delta gives the answer. For example, the delta on a far out-of-the-money call option might be something like .01. If traders had studied the delta before making the trade, they would have realized that if the stock goes up a dollar, the option will only go up a penny. If you look at the delta before you buy, you'll see that cheap out-of-the-money options are truly a long shot. In extreme cases, the stock goes up $3 and the option might not gain anything.

Some traders make rules for themselves. For example, they might only buy an option if the delta is .7 or higher (it's obviously in-the-money). You really have to experiment before you can make any hard-and-fast rules. For example, on a stock like Google, you might have to be in-the-money by 50 points before the delta is .7. On the other hand, on a stock like GE, a delta of .7 can be attained after one strike price in-the-money.

Obviously, an entire chapter could be written about delta and delta trading techniques. For example, many pros use *delta neutral* strategies such as straddles, designed to be profitable no matter which way the underlying stock moves. In addition, when looking at the relationship between the underlying stock and option (discussed in Chapter 14), the delta tells you how big a move the option is really making rather than what it appears to be making.

The Bottom Line: Delta, as well as the other Greeks, is something that cannot be ignored.

Note: Your brokerage firm or the OIC will give you the delta on any option if you call and ask.

. . . .

Now that you've been introduced to straddles and spreads, you'll learn how to sell naked puts, as well as how to trade the strangle.

16

Selling Naked Puts and the Strangle

In this chapter we're going to discuss what it means to sell options naked. Now you know the truth. Options traders actually have a sense of humor! As you remember, when you first sold covered calls back in Part Two, you owned the underlying stock. It was physically in your brokerage account. Your position is said to be protected or covered. If the underlying stock goes down, you won't owe any money because the underlying stock is safely in your account. You can hold onto it until the stock recovers (or in the worst case, goes to zero).

On the other hand, if you sell a *naked* (or *uncovered*) call or put, it means you don't own the underlying stock. How can you sell something that you don't own? It's also why you'll need a margin agreement if you want to sell calls or puts. By the way, people also refer to this strategy as *writing puts*.

Selling naked puts is actually an intriguing strategy and can be a useful tool if used properly. Unfortunately, some people don't use options properly, which is why this strategy has so many restrictions. By the time you get to this level (Level 4), you are into some very serious options trading. The brokerage firm will likely not let you sell naked unless you can prove you know what you're doing. By the time you finish this chapter, however, you should have a better idea of whether this strategy will work for you.

Note: You'll notice that we're not going to discuss selling naked calls, a strategy done so rarely that it's not worth our time to review it. (It's also incredibly risky.) Selling naked puts, although risky, actually does make sense under certain circumstances and is a rather popular strategy with experienced options traders.

Warning: These strategies are extremely dangerous to your financial well-being and are not recommended for first-time investors. Proceed at your own risk. Feel free to skip to Part Six if you are sure you'll never use the strategies included in this chapter. On the other hand, you might enjoy reading the chapter simply for the entertaining stories.

What It Means to Sell Naked (or Uncovered) Puts

The definition of *selling naked puts* (or *uncovered put writing*) comes from Investopedia.com: "A put option whose writer does not have a short position in the stock on which he or she has written the put."

Another definition from the Options Industry Council (OIC): "A short put option position in which the writer does not have a corresponding short position in the underlying security or has not deposited, in a cash account, cash or cash equivalents equal to the exercise value of the put."

In other words, when you sell naked puts, you are hoping that the stock goes up. I know this sounds strange but think of it this way. When you *buy* puts, you are taking a short position, so you want the underlying stock to go down. When you *sell* puts, you are selling a short position, so you want the underlying stock to go up.

One of the reasons that selling naked is attractive to traders is it's a way of leveraging other people's money into substantial profits (or so they hope). When you sell a put, you are paid a premium. That's right. You are getting cash from the buyer, and you don't even own the stock. That's why speculators like this strategy. You are using this strategy to receive revenue on stocks you don't own.

Ideally, the underlying stock stays the same or goes up. Then you pocket the premium on the expiration date. This is what you hope for.

You receive premium on a stock that you don't even own. It almost sounds too good to be true. When you see it on paper, it seems even better than selling covered calls.

Why You Would Sell Puts

There are two reasons why you would sell puts: you are either a speculator or a strategist.

1. *Speculator*: You can use this strategy to bring in additional income from stocks you don't own. Keep in mind you must have the cash equivalent in your account (like stocks) or cash to use this strategy. You hope that the underlying stock stays the same or goes up in price, allowing you to keep the premium you received.
2. *Strategist*: The second reason to sell puts is to bring in income while planning a stock purchase. In other words, a strategist can sell puts as a method to enter the stock market and buy stocks at a discount.

When the Stock Gets "Put" to You

One of the unique features of selling naked puts and the reason the strategy is risky is that the stock can get "put" to you, or given to you. The official term is that the stock is *assigned* to you.

If you are using the strategy for speculation, the last thing you want is the stock placed in your account, or assigned. You just want the revenue from selling the put. But if the stock goes down, not up, then you could find yourself in trouble. What you really want is for the option to expire worthless and to never hit the strike price.

If you are assigned the stock, you are required or obligated by the rules to buy the stock at the strike price. Let's summarize what all of this means. You have received money for selling a put option on a stock that you don't own. That is your monetary reward. But by the rules of the contract, you are also required to buy the stock at the strike price (if the option is exercised, that is).

For example, let's say you sold puts on Tracking, Inc., that is now trading for $40 a share. You are pretty comfortable with this company and believe—based on its trading history—that it won't go much below $40 a share. So you sell a naked put on Tracking, Inc., at a strike price of $35. In other words, if the stock stays above $35 a share, you're in good shape. And even if the stock goes higher, you still receive the premium from selling the put.

But what if you are wrong or something unexpected happens? What if the stock pulled an Enron and fell by 80 percent before the expiration date? What if the stock fell to $30 a share? What would happen is you would be assigned the stock at $35 a share. You would be required to buy it at $35 a share no matter how low the stock fell. Therefore, the stock would be "put" in your account (it will probably be assigned upon expiration), sold to you at $35 a share. You have an immediate 5-point loss, and perhaps more if the stock keeps falling.

If you're a speculator, the last thing you wanted was to put Tracking, Inc., in your account. You didn't want to tie up your money with a stock purchase. So being forced to buy this stock at $35 was an unwelcome development.

If You're Not Speculating

If you're not speculating and had actually planned on buying this $40 stock at $35 a share, then selling naked puts can make sense. Instead of speculating, you are strategizing.

For example, let's say that your target price for buying Tracking, Inc., was $35 a share. Based on technical and fundamental analysis, you have determined this is a reasonable price for the stock. You don't want to pay anything more than $35 a share. So you sell a naked put at the strike price of $35.

First, you receive revenue or premium from selling the put. This way you can bring in revenue while you are waiting for Tracking, Inc., to hit your target price. And if the stock falls to $35, as you assumed it would, the stock will be assigned and will be placed in your brokerage account. Guess what? Unlike the speculator, you don't mind owning Tracking, Inc. In fact, that was part of your trading plan.

Obviously, if the stock continued to fall, it wouldn't be pleasant, but you were planning on buying it anyway. As a strategist, you are willing to hold on to the stock for the long term. Unlike the speculator, you don't mind having your money tied up. It was part of your plan to own Tracking, Inc. In this case, selling naked puts can actually make sense, assuming your calculations are correct. By selling puts, the premium you receive will reduce the price you paid for the shares.

Let's see what happens in real life. The underlying stock, Tracking, Inc., flops around for a while, going as high as $43 a share. Ideally, Tracking, Inc., will never drop to the strike price, and the option expires worthless. Then you could sell another naked put for the following month.

If by the expiration date, Tracking, Inc., is still above the strike price of $35, you keep the premium and the put option expires worthless. You basically received money for assuming the risk. This is actually an ideal outcome.

But let's say a couple of weeks before expiration, Tracking, Inc., drops from $40 to $32 on bad news. You wake up the following Monday morning and discover the stock has been assigned, or "put," to you at the $35 strike price. According to the terms of the options contract, you are required to buy Tracking, Inc., at $35 and the shares are placed in your account. You still get to keep the premium. However, it is little compensation for the 3-point loss.

Managing Assignment

If you are assigned (and you will eventually be assigned if the stock price is below the strike price), and you are forced to buy the stock, here are your three choices.

1. *Hold*: You can hold the stock indefinitely until it reaches your long-term target price.
2. *Sell*: You could immediately sell the stock, letting the premium you received help offset the loss from getting assigned.
3. *Backup strategy*: Another strategy is to turn around and sell a covered call on the stock, bringing in additional revenue. This is your backup strategy in case you are assigned a sinking stock and will also offset any potential loss from assignment. With this strategy, you are receiving premium twice, first from selling the naked put and then from selling a covered call.

Note: Before you are assigned the stock, you have another choice, especially in an emergency. You could buy back the put contract you sold because you want to avoid assignment. In this case, if you see the stock dropping, you take the loss now by buying back the put contract.

The Ideal Stock for Selling Puts

You are looking for stocks that are going to go up. If you believe the stock will go up a lot, you might as well buy the underlying stock or buy calls. In the past, some traders did well by selling puts on stocks like Intel, Microsoft, and GE. Other choices include financial stocks that moved up slowly and also paid a hefty dividend. So even if you were assigned, you would receive dividend payments.

The Risks of Selling Naked Puts

It's actually fascinating to talk about the risks of selling naked puts because so many things can go wrong. There were moments in stock market history—1929, 1987, and 2000—that destroyed the accounts of put sellers.

On the days that the stock market crashes, put sellers are especially vulnerable. They are suddenly being assigned stocks that are falling quickly. Although these really bad days don't happen too often, individual stocks routinely fall every day, and that's when speculators selling naked puts wished they had come up with another strategy. If some bad news comes out on the stock, it will seriously affect your purchase.

The reason that selling naked is a risky strategy is that people use it for speculation. In this case, it can be hazardous to your finances, especially if you are assigned. You have to make a lot of calculations to prepare for the possible risks. It's not a good sign when you need a calculator to determine all the things that could go wrong.

Selling naked puts is not the kind of strategy you initiate right before you go on vacation. If you do, you might not have an account when you get back. It's also not the kind of strategy you can put on autopilot. You have to closely monitor the underlying stock.

If used properly, selling naked puts can make sense for sophisticated and experienced traders who are willing to thoroughly research the underlying stock and market conditions. Nevertheless, some people have been talked into using this strategy without being fully aware of the risk that they could lose more money than they started with. That is why some pros recommend that you not sell naked options under any circumstances.

How My Friend Got Put

I don't want to completely scare you out of selling naked puts, but you should be fully aware of the potential risks. Many options traders believe that selling naked puts is the best strategy without fully appreciating what could go wrong.

One of my experienced trader friends, Robert (not his real name), told me his true story. "General Motors (NY: GM) had dropped from $45 a share to $28 a share," he said. "I assumed from my studies that it had reached a bottom, and that solid, intelligent investors were investing in the stock. So I sold to open the put at a $25 strike price with two months out. I did it to speculate and to receive the revenue."

He didn't think that GM would go lower than $25 a share, which is why he selected a $25 strike price. "I thought I had a 3-point buffer. Then everything fell apart. First, Delphi, the parts supplier for GM, declared bankruptcy. Then the United Auto Workers pressured General Motors for further coverage in their pension plan. GM didn't have enough money to cover all of the retirees."

So the stock dropped from $28 a share to $19. It happened so fast he didn't have time to buy the put back to close the position. "I was assigned at $25 a share and the put contract was closed. This means I bought GM at $25 a share with significant losses. Now I anticipate holding GM for 5 or 10 years."

Robert says that, on paper, selling puts seems like a very effective strategy. But once you are assigned, you wish you hadn't done it.

A Retiree Gets Wiped Out

Robert is not the only one who got caught on the wrong side of this strategy. I had a conversation with a Home Depot employee. He was well past retirement age. In fact, he had retired years ago to dabble in options. He told me that through most of the 1980s he was selling millions of dollars worth of naked puts in his account. For many years, the strategy was quite effective.

Unfortunately, the more money he and his friends made, the more risks they began to take. Often, they'd sell as many puts as the brokerage firm allowed. In those days, margin requirements were looser, so many speculators relied heavily on margin to buy more stocks and options than they could afford.

In October 1987, the market fell by over 20 percent in one day. Although most people fled the market for safer investments, put sellers were forced to buy back losing stocks at high strike prices. Some speculators didn't have enough money in their account to cover the huge losses, so they immediately received margin calls.

When the accounts cleared a few days later, many put sellers were wiped out, including the gentleman who worked at Home Depot. He went from being a millionaire to being broke in less than a week. He told me he'll be working at Home Depot for the rest of his life, all because he risked too much money using this strategy, and didn't plan for the worst-case scenario.

The Strangle

Although a strangle is technically a Level 3 options strategy, it does involve selling or buying naked, which is why I left it for the end of the chapter. A strangle can be long or short depending on your strategy. A long strangle is similar to a straddle—you buy a call and put with different strike prices. To make money with a long strangle, you want the underlying stock to make a really huge move.

With a short strangle, however, you don't want the underlying stock to move at all. To be precise, a short strangle consists of selling a call out-of-the-money and selling a put out-of-the-money with the same underlying stock and expiration date. The strike price, however, is different. If this is the first time you've heard about a strangle, it will seem unusual, at least at first.

For example, let's say that General Electric (NY: GE) has been trading in a range between $32 and $34. You determine through technical analysis that GE won't be trading out of this range in the near future. So you initiate a short strangle, selling the January 35 call and selling the January 30 put. Because you are selling the call and selling the put, you are receiving premium from both legs. The strangle works best on stocks that are not going anywhere (thus the name, strangle, as if you are choking). By the way, if you do a strangle on a volatile stock, you are the one who could get strangled.

There are two possible outcomes. GE remains at or around $34 a share and you keep the premium. Perhaps you received $0.50 for selling the 35 call and $0.35 for selling the 30 put. Your premium will be low for low volatile stocks. If you had chosen more volatile stocks, you'd receive additional premium but also put yourself at greater risk.

If GE stays between $32 and $34, you'll get to keep the premium as both options expire. But what if GE suddenly drops to $29 a share? Then the premium on the put goes up while the premium on the call goes down. You'd have to use the money you received from the premium to buy back your option. You'll have to work hard to unwind the position. In the worst-case scenario, the stock goes up or down 10 points and you are stuck with two losing legs.

The question you have to ask yourself is this: why would you take on a complex trade with limited revenue and unlimited loss? After all, in the worst-case scenario, the stock will be put to you, and you'll be looking at significant losses. Remember, whenever you sell a naked option, there is always the danger you will be assigned the stock, so potential losses could be substantial.

Perhaps if you find the most docile stock in a slow-moving market, it would make sense. As one of my friends said, "If you think selling naked is bad—with the short strangle you are double-naked." And it's true. You are naked on both sides. Professional traders who do these kinds of trades all day long know how to cover both sides when they are wrong. If you are a novice trader, it's best if you avoid this strategy until you gain a lot more experience.

The Black-Scholes
Options Pricing Model

History

All professional options traders are familiar with the Black-Scholes options pricing model. Before Black-Scholes, there was no reliable way of calculating the fair value of a stock option. Unfortunately, understanding the mathematical formulas for the value of put and call options really is rocket science. Many consider options pricing the most complex area of finance.

The good news is there is computer software that will give you the results you need without your having to obtain a degree in advanced calculus. Although you must know the factors that influence options premiums, it's not essential you learn the formulas for constructing and pricing options (unless you are planning on becoming a professional trader or work in the securities industry).

The report on the European options pricing equation was published by Fisher Black and Myron Scholes in 1973, improving on ideas published by Robert Merton and Paul Samuelson from the University of Chicago. In turn, these men based their work on a number of imperfect options pricing theories and dissertations that were previously published.

When Black and Scholes joined forces, they created a remarkably accurate pricing model. Many consider it the most important concept in modern financial theory. (At first, their paper was rejected by several academic journals.) As a result of their work, they received the Nobel Prize in 1997, although Black had died two years earlier. Even now, when you talk about options trading, it's likely the Black-Scholes options pricing formula will be mentioned.

How Black-Scholes Works

Black-Scholes (and other options pricing models such as the Cox, Ross and Rubinstein model) are mathematical formulas that price an options contract. You input known variables such as the price of the underlying security, days left to expiration, the strike price, dividends, interest rates, and the important one: the historic volatility of the underlying stock.

After entering these known variables, Black-Scholes will give you the fair value of the options contract, displayed as a percentage. This percentage is the market's expectation of volatility in the underlying security. It's an attempt to predict what is going to happen to the underlying security, that is, how much it is going to move.

The entire purpose of an options pricing model is to determine whether or not the option is fairly priced. For example, if the pricing model says that the theoretical value of the option is $4 but the market says the option is worth $5, the market is *implying* that the stock is going to be more volatile. So who's right, the market or the pricing model?

Ask any pro. The market is always right, and the difference of opinion is what makes the market. It's up to the individual trader to decide whether he or she is willing to pay more for an option than it's worth. Individual traders must weigh the risk and reward before they make the trade. Options pricing models like Black-Scholes tell you whether an option is fairly valued or not, but it doesn't tell you what to do about it. Options models are especially useful to market makers on the floor of the exchange who make a living out of pricing options.

. . . .

Now that you've been introduced to advanced level options trading, you're entering the opinion section of this book. Although it's often beneficial to listen to other people's opinions, in the end you are responsible for your own decisions.

With that in mind, in the next chapter you are going to read a fascinating interview I had with Sheldon Natenberg on the importance of volatility in options trading. You might also gain some additional insights into the mind of a professional trader.

PART SIX

UNCOMMON
ADVICE

Sheldon Natenberg: Professional Options Trader

If you ask professional traders for the title of one of the most influential books about options, more than likely Natenberg's book *Option Volatility & Pricing: Advanced Trading Strategies and Techniques* (McGraw-Hill, 1994) will be mentioned. Although geared primarily to the professional trader, his insights into the importance of volatility to determine option prices were a breakthrough in the options world.

Natenberg started his career as an independent market maker in equity options at the Chicago Board Options Exchange (CBOE) before later moving to the floor of the Chicago Board of Trade (CBOT). I caught up with Natenberg when he was between classes. Since 2000, he has been the director of education in charge of training professional options traders for the Chicago Trading Company, a proprietary derivatives trading firm.

What is the most common misconception about options?

The big problem for all options traders, including professionals, is this idea of volatility, the speed of the market. If someone thinks the market is going up, he or she will tend to buy calls. And if it turns out these people are right, and the market did go up, they might end up losing money. Why did they lose money? Buying calls is supposed to be a bullish position, and the market went up. But of course what was happening is the market was going up slowly, not sufficiently fast enough to offset the decay in the option. This idea of volatility is unique to options markets, but it is the overriding consideration in many strategies.

So should retail traders be aware of volatility?

There are two things you can trade on in the options markets. You can trade on the direction of the market—you have an opinion that the market is going up or down. Or you can trade on the speed of the market, which is volatility. How fast is the market going to move? Two typical volatility strategies are a straddle or strangle.

Most professional options traders have decided they're not very good at picking the direction of the market so they focus on the other characteristic: the speed of the market. Generally, people focus on one or the other. For retail customers, I think direction is the most important consideration. Most professional traders trade on volatility.

In my opinion, a nonprofessional needs to combine a price outlook with an understanding of volatility, and it's not easy. It's hard enough just to deal with the price, but to deal with the price and volatility together is more than most people are willing to do. If someone is really good at picking the direction of the market, my feeling is forget about options and buy or sell the stock.

Can you explain volatility so a novice can understand it?

You could say there are two basic interpretations. One is the volatility of the underlying market. Is the stock moving $5 a day or $1 a day, $0.05 a day, $0.10 a day or sitting still? The other idea is implied volatility, which is what the marketplace thinks is going to happen, and this is what determines options prices.

Here's an example that we use a lot in our business. You're trying to figure out what to wear when you are getting up in the morning. In other words, you're trying to figure out what the weather is going to be today. Obviously, it's the future weather.

Let's say you think it's going to be sunny because that's what the weather report said. You look out the window and everyone is carrying an umbrella. What are they saying? They are implying through their actions what they think the weather is going to be. And basically, when you trade, you are betting your judgment against the marketplace's judgment. You're betting it's not going to rain even though everyone is carrying an umbrella.

Let's relate it to options trading. The marketplace thinks that certain things are going to happen and they price options accordingly. The price of the option is based on what people think will happen. And what they think is going to happen can be translated into volatility—an implied volatility.

So you use volatility to determine the value of an option?

Exactly. The value of an option in theory is dependent on the volatility of the underlying market—how fast it moves. What traders try to do is try to make their best estimate of what the volatility is going to be over the life of the option—that is, how much the underlying stock is going to move around.

The actual volatility, which no one can know, will determine the value of the option. Perhaps I can put it this way. Everything that is traded—it doesn't matter whether it is options or anything else—is a question of price versus value. If you see something with a high value and a low price, you want to be a buyer. Something with a high price and a low value, you want to be a seller.

Options traders are making the same judgments, but we calculate the value using a theoretical pricing model like Black-Scholes. The theoretical pricing model requires us to make a judgment about the volatility of the underlying market over the life of the option.

However, we can work backwards and say, "Suppose I know the price. What volatility does the marketplace imply by looking at this price?" Traders usually think of the theoretical value as being the volatility over the life of the option. They think of the price as being the implied volatility.

Can a novice use that to his or her advantage?

Anyone in options trading should be familiar with the basics of theoretical pricing. The question is how do you use it? If most retail traders think the market is going up, there are several things they can do. They can certainly buy the stock. They can also buy calls. The question is should they buy calls or not? They should be buying calls if they think the calls give them an advantage.

For example, if retail traders use a model that says the call is worth $6, and it's trading for $4, in theory they have a $2 advantage in buying the calls. Once they have made the trade, they would treat it differently than would a professional, who would do certain types of hedging. In the long run, the retail trader would still come out better by buying the calls. If the calls were $6, and the price is $6, they might as well just buy the stock.

Most retail customers start with an idea that a stock is going up or down. And they have a directional opinion. The next question is if they should take advantage of their directional opinion in the options market. They can use a theoretical pricing model like Black-Scholes to do that.

How does a pricing model like Black-Scholes work?

Assuming the input is correct, the model gives you a value for the option. The trader will compare it to the price in the marketplace and decide whether he or she should be buying or selling. The difficult part is you have to enter a volatility number. Most traders look at graphs of volatility from the past (historical volatility) to come up with a prediction of the future.

What conclusions did you make about volatility and pricing?

The simple answer is people don't pay enough attention to it. They don't realize how dramatically options can be affected by changes in volatility. It's confusing because volatility is unique to options trading and is something most people have never come across before. You watch the evening newscast, and they say the market is really volatile today. The options trader asks: How do you quantify that? What number says that the market is more or less volatile?

I will give you an example. The idea of volatility is based on the assumption that the world looks like a bell-shaped curve. In other words, if you graphed the distribution of price changes, in theory they should look like a bell-shaped curve. The question you have to ask is: Is that true? And everyone knows it isn't true.

Volatility is another name for standard deviation. If you look in a textbook, sometimes it won't say volatility but will say standard deviation. But of course the standard deviation is based on the assumption you are working with a normal distribution: a bell-shaped curve. Nothing that we trade is exactly a normal distribution. So everyone is trying to make adjustments to make the model better fit the real world. What is the probability of the underlying stock going to this level, which will cause the option to be worth this? The options pricing models are just probability-based models. If you get the probabilities correct, you will get the value correct.

How do the pros manage risk?

If you looked at a professional trading firm, went in, and analyzed what the traders are doing, you'd find they are spending a lot more time worrying about the risk of the position they have taken than trying to figure out exactly whether they got the right values in the marketplace. Perhaps the biggest mistake made by traders is the lack of risk management. People are not sufficiently sensitive to the ways that market conditions can change and how that can affect options.

Think of Long-Term Capital Management [a narrative of the rise and fall of this hedge fund can be found in Chapter 9]. These guys were as smart as they come. And they were primarily trading on relationships and volatility and their losses were significant.

How could that happen?

In our business, the intelligent trading of options from a purely pro's point of view requires people to focus on two things. Number one, how do you figure out what an option is worth? Do you use a Black-Scholes model or some other model? But all those models are based on the laws of probability. The fact is, you can have all the probabilities right and still lose money—because you can be unlucky in the short run.

You hear about all the bad things that happen to individual traders and firms—it's mainly a lack of discipline. Everyone makes mistakes. Number two, can you accept your mistake, take your loss, and go on? Some people just can't accept their mistake and make it worse and worse.

I'm thinking of Nick Leeson (the futures trader who single-handedly wiped out the 233-year-old Baring Investment Bank). From what I read, he is not a bad person. He just started to lose money for the firm in a way that he wasn't supposed to, and his ego wouldn't let him admit what was happening.

So how do you plan for what could go wrong?

It's not just asking what bad things can happen but it's also asking what action to take if you run into bad luck. You must be prepared. If you're not prepared, then you freeze. That's happened to almost every trader. Things go against you, and you hadn't thought about it, and you have no idea what you are going to do. And it's not only the bad luck. Professional traders also ask: If things go my way and I get really fortunate, what should I do to maximize my profits? It's not only what I am going to do to minimize my losses when things go bad, but what I am going to do to maximize my profits when things go well.

Does software help?

You couldn't trade options without the software—it is invaluable. But you also can't be a slave to the software. The software isn't any good unless you understand what is behind it. For example, you can get software that tells you what an option is worth under certain conditions. And what makes these models like Black-Scholes really valuable is that you can ask: What if conditions change in this way. How will my position work or how will it look? You have to consider a wide variety of possibilities. You can't plan for every scenario, but you have to broaden your horizon beyond what people normally do.

I will use the software to determine how my position will look if the market price changes, if volatility changes, if time passes, if interest rates change. All of these different things can occur in the market. You have to ask yourself what worries you the most. And what am I going to do if things start to go against me?

Is it better to buy options on indexes or on stocks?

We find it's easier to trade index options than individual equities, although we do trade individual equities. You have to do a lot more research with equities. It really depends on how you are trying to trade. A professional market making firm wants to make a lot of small profits on a large turnover, whereas the average retail trader is trying to make a large profit on a small turnover.

As one trader said, "Professional trading is like picking up dimes in front of a bulldozer. You can make a lot of money but you better keep your eye on the bulldozer." You'll get run over if you don't.

We trade on high volume. We try to make money from the bid-offer spread, buying at the bid and selling at the offer. We're happy to make small profit many times over whereas a retail customer wants to buy the next hot stock. For us, it's easier to hit a lot of singles in the index markets or interest rate markets because the characteristics of these markets are easier to deal with.

What other advice would you give traders?

The most important advice, which I also give to the pros, is that you should learn as many strategies as possible. You should go out and do every possible strategy you ever learned, but you should do it really small. If you go out and do one or two contracts, you will not get killed. By doing them in the real world, you will learn a lot. The problem with a lot of traders, even the pros, is they get a little knowledge and want to trade in bigger sizes, and they don't realize the bad things that can happen.

I'm not trying to discourage anyone from trading options, because I think it's a fascinating field. But you have to be realistic. It's not easy and there is a lot to learn. At our firm, Chicago Trading Company, you will learn for at least a year before they even let you trade.

Is there a secret the pros know that we don't?

No! Occasionally I see an ad in the paper that announces someone is coming to town and invites readers to learn the secrets of the pros. There are no secrets. The only secret is hard work.

Most retail customers look at options trading as a hobby. There is nothing wrong with that, but you can't expect to be as good as a professional trader if you're not willing to put in the time and effort. A pro will put in more time and effort because his or her livelihood depends on it.

Let's say someone reads your book and wants to trade professionally?

Regardless of how good a book is, it can't give you all the aspects of trading unless you go into the real world and do it yourself. It's like taking a class. No matter how good the instructor, no matter how good the class—it just gives you a foundation to go into the real world, but it doesn't give you every unique situation you are going to encounter.

But you have to follow the first rule of beginning trading. Do it small. Whatever you do, do it small, that is until you understand the different things that can occur and the relationships between options and different strategies.

What does it take to be a successful trader?

From the professional point of view, you have to be good with numbers. You don't have to be a mathematician, but you have to manipulate numbers quickly. We found in options trading that people who like probability-based games like chess, bridge, or poker tend to do well in options because they can appreciate the different probabilities and the way things fit together.

To be successful in this business, you have to be disciplined and willing to accept losses. You also have to make new decisions every day. Let's say I buy a stock at $100 and the stock is now at $98. I have to forget about whether I should have bought the stock at $100. I have to put yesterday's decision behind me and look at the new conditions today. Maybe I think the stock is going up. Maybe I think I should buy more stock. Or perhaps I realized I made a mistake, take my $2 loss, and look for another stock. The minute you fall asleep, however, is when the market comes up and bites you.

Trading Index Options

Indexes are basically a basket or portfolio of stocks that are grouped together in a particular way. When you buy index options, you are participating in the market that consists of the components of that index. Indexes include the NDX (Nasdaq 100), the DJX (Dow Jones Industrial Average Index), the SPX (S&P 500), as well as more specialized indexes such as the XAU (PHLX Gold and Silver Index), to name just a few. There are hundreds of indexes available for trading.

In 2006, the CBOE also introduced an index option on the Chicago Board Options Exchange Volatility Index (VIX), which measures the volatility of the U.S. stock market by tracking the S&P 500 options contracts. That's right, you are buying options on options, or to be more specific, you are literally buying options on volatility.

Many pros trade index options to protect their portfolios from short-term drops or to juice up their stock positions. It's a cheap and efficient way of participating in the broad market without having to buy individual stocks.

For the individual, it's a lot cheaper to buy index options than to buy an entire basket of stock indexes (which is expensive). If you are convinced the market is headed in one direction or another, buying index options allows you to easily and cheaply participate.

Although index options are relatively easy to trade, they do behave differently than traditional options. For example, many index options cease trading on the Thursday before Expiration Friday. Another unusual feature is that they can only be exercised at expiration (although there are exceptions).

As usual, you should start out trading indexes cautiously with a minimal number of contracts until you gain more experience. Each index trades differently. For example, the NDX will likely be more volatile than the DJX.

The disadvantages of index options are the same as with standard options. First, they do expire, which means you have to be right about the direction and timing of the underlying index to be profitable. In addition, some broad indexes like the DJX may move more slowly so although you might be right about the direction, the index doesn't move fast enough to make any money. There are other factors at play (for example, the spread) which can affect whether you'll be profitable.

Can individuals make money trading index options? Yes, but you shouldn't wake up one morning and say, "I want to trade indexes." Instead, you could wait for a market event (perhaps a sell-off) to buy index options. If you are buying calls, the market has to be low and on its way up. You could use the powerful 50-day moving average to determine when to enter or exit the index.

The Spread on Index Options

You will find that the spreads on index options are often wider, which is why market makers like trading them. As an index buyer, you must be cautious of the spread in an index option because it can often be significant. For example, the bid-ask spread might be $1.00 (bid price) by $1.10 (ask price) on a particular index. As the index becomes more volatile, the spread might change to $1.00 by $1.30. The market makers, based on their very sophisticated computer models, determine the price they can be profitable. As the index becomes more volatile, they may increase the spread to safeguard their profit margin. No matter what index you are trading, it's essential you pay close attention to the spread.

· ·

Now that you've gotten some insights into how a professional thinks and trades, the last chapter contains my list of recommended books and seminars, as well as my opinion about expensive options seminars.

What I Really Think about Options

After researching, trading, and studying options for several years, I have a few observations that might be helpful. You may or may not agree with my conclusions, but keep in mind they are my opinions. Let's begin by looking at some of the places you can go if you need additional help, or, better yet, if you want to pursue an even more advanced options education.

Where to Get Help

Phone Numbers

1-888-OPTIONS (1-888-678-4667)

This is the phone number of the Options Industry Council (OIC), the educational arm of all six U.S. options exchanges and the Options Clearing Corporation (OCC). If you have questions about trading options while reading my book, this is *the* number to call. The staff is extremely knowledgeable and helpful (but don't call for investment advice). You can also e-mail questions to options@theocc.com.

Online Resources

www.888options.com

This is the Web site of the OIC, an excellent site filled with educational material and free options quotes. In addition, they offer free online options training, and free classes and seminars. They also have special options calculators that give you important variables, such as implied volatility and delta.

www.cboe.com

This is the Web site of the Chicago Board Options Exchange (CBOE), an excellent site containing free options quotes. They also offer online options training, inexpensive classes, and seminars. The site is filled with educational information, including special calculators that do complex analysis. In addition, if you want to learn more about the tax ramifications of trading options, download a copy of the brochure, "Taxes & Investing," from this site.

www.investopedia.com

This useful Web site, designed like an encyclopedia, helps novice traders understand complicated terms about anything related to investing and trading.

finance.yahoo.com

Select the options tab and you'll enter a world of message boards, options calculators, and detailed examples of options strategies.

www.optionstradermag.com

You can download a copy of *Options Trader*, a well-regarded options magazine at the above Web address. The monthly magazine is loaded with useful articles, news, trader interviews, and important options events. It's aimed at the intermediate and advanced trader—published by *Active Trader* magazine.

Options Software

Most of the large brokerage firms have software that compares, analyzes, and evaluates options and options strategies. More than likely, you can get the software for free when you open up an account. If not, both the CBOE and the OIC have online option calculators that will probably meet most of your immediate needs.

In addition, the OIC has a *free* educational software package, Options Investigator, which allows you to enter "what if" options scenarios before you buy or sell. They'll send the software to you in the mail if you call.

Additional Reading

For Beginners

Reminiscences of a Stock Operator (Wiley, 1994) by Edwin Lefevre

One of the best books on trading stocks as seen through the eyes of master speculator Jesse Livermore. Although primarily geared to trading stocks, the psychological lessons Livermore learned are required reading for all traders.

New Insights on Covered Call Writing (Bloomberg Press, 2003) by Richard Lehman and Lawrence McMillan

A very readable book on selling covered calls. If you are interested in learning even more details about this strategy, this is a good place to start.

Intermediate to Advanced Trading

Characteristics and Risks of Standardized Options

This is the must-read brochure published by the Options Clearing Corporation (OCC) that can be found for free on the OCC or CBOE Web site. The brochure is required reading for options traders, although it's a bit technical.

Options (McGraw-Hill, 1999) by The Options Institute

This book on options trading is published by the CBOE. The book contains useful information about strategies and what goes on behind the scenes at the exchanges.

Options as a Strategic Investment (Prentice-Hall, 2001) by
Lawrence G. McMillan

This 900-page classic is used as a textbook in many college classrooms. It's not as technical as other advanced-level options books, so it's an easier read, and is still a must-read for anyone pursuing a career as a professional options trader.

Professional Trading

Options, Futures and Other Derivatives (Prentice Hall, 2005) by
John C. Hull

The sixth edition of this classic 800-page book is considered the bible of options and derivatives. The author is a recognized expert in the field and gives many examples of how options are constructed and priced.

*Option Volatility & Pricing: Advanced Trading Strategies and
Techniques* (McGraw-Hill, 1994) by Sheldon Natenberg

A thought-provoking book on the effect of volatility when pricing options. Recommended reading if you are going to pursue professional-level options trading.

Seminars and Classes

www.888options.com

The OIC Web site includes loads of educational material and useful information. They also offer free online classes and free seminars throughout the country that teach you the basics as well as advanced strategies. The best part is they teach you what you need to know for free without any strings attached.

www.cboe.com

You can sign up for relatively inexpensive classes (from $50 to $700) that will teach you what you need to know about options, from beginning to advanced strategies.

Continuing Education Classes

Check your local college or high school for reasonably priced options classes. The colleges either teach options as a separate course or include it as part of a finance class. In addition, if you are preparing for a broker's license, Series 7, you will need to be thoroughly familiar with constructing and pricing options. Many schools offer Series 7 classes, which include a detailed options discussion.

What about High-priced Options Classes for Retail Traders?

In my opinion, you should think twice about attending high-priced classes for retail investors that charge between $4,000 and $30,000 (or $15,000 if you sign up today) for two- to five-day classes to teach strategies that you can learn in this book.

The instructors at these classes mainly teach speculative strategies that are designed to make money when you have little or no money. They also lead you to believe that the more complicated the strategy and the sexier the name, the more money you'll make. So the only way you can be profitable is by taking additional classes and buying their software.

I was invited to a free workshop designed to convince me (and 30 other attendees) to sign up for an expensive options seminar. The instructor literally said anything to get us to sign the four-page contract. He justified the $4,000 cost for the seminar by reminding us that we'll spend at least that much money on a big screen television set. "And we can guarantee you'll make all your money back within a year of trading," the instructor promised the crowd.

Actually, the funniest thing the instructor said was that we shouldn't read books on options trading because we won't remember what we read. The second funniest thing he said was that they only teach low-risk, high-return strategies in the seminars.

At the workshop, the instructor said the secret to successful trading involves buying cheap out-of-the-money call options on low volatile stocks like Wal-Mart a few weeks before earnings are announced—and selling as soon as the stock goes up 2, 3, or 4 points. "You can make $3,780 in one day!" he shouted.

I asked this question: "What is the probability of a low volatile stock like Wal-Mart going up that many points after an earnings announcement?" His answer: "I'll get back to you later." He added, "But you can always do a bull call spread." *Note to Instructor*: It's been years since Wal-Mart went up more than a point after an earnings announcement. And a bull call spread won't save you.

My View

What do I think? Many brokerage firms and Internet Web sites have sophisticated options software programs that can search for multiple criteria and do advanced option calculations—provided free to customers. Call your brokerage firm and see what it offers or search the Internet. So before you plunk down thousands of dollars for software that purports to tell you the best time to buy and sell, use the free software provided by your brokerage firm.

There is also a difference between attending a school that teaches options trading and a seminar that helps you learn speculative strategies. Learning how to trade options is not as simple as buying a software program. If someone really did create a software package that magically picked the options to buy or sell, he or she wouldn't share it with you or me.

In addition, how can these software programs (as well as Web-based services that are offered for a monthly fee) compete with the million-dollar programs provided by brokerage firms or options exchanges? The truth is there is no secret system that will make you rich. The leaders often ask, "How much money do you want to make?" You should immediately answer: "How much money could I lose?"

At the seminars, people are always intrigued by spreads. The selling point is that you are using the premium from one leg to finance the other leg. You are buying and selling multiple options with every possible position covered. Everything works brilliantly in the classroom, but in the real world of trading, it doesn't turn out so perfectly.

In the classroom, under laboratory conditions, it's very easy to find the exact options that fit your strategy. In real life, finding options that fit the criteria you are looking for is a lot harder than you think. And the more complex the strategy, the harder it is to control the variables. There is one basic truth that many instructors fail to tell you. Many speculators lose money, although the exact number is hard to pinpoint. On the other hand, you can do very well if you use options as part of a planned strategy to increase income or as a method to buy stocks.

Another truth is that many people think that the more expensive something is, the more valuable it is. Therefore, you probably believe that the $30,000 class will be more beneficial than a free course. Unless you are thinking of being a professional working on the floor of the exchange, you should be very cautious about enrolling in those over-priced classes that you can get for almost free at one of the options exchanges, your brokerage firm, an online Internet class, or a community college.

In my opinion, if you want to continue your education, you can do much better by taking classes offered at the CBOE and the OIC. They will teach you the skills you need for thousands of dollars less.

What I Really Think about Trading Options

Just as I believe people should learn about, and participate in, the stock market, people should learn about, and participate in, the options market. There are times when you need options for all of the reasons I've mentioned in this book: income, speculation, hedging, and insurance. If used properly, options are an excellent way to manage your portfolio and increase your returns.

In my opinion, you should start by selling covered calls. If you ask me whether I'd rather be the options buyer or options seller, I would choose options seller. That way, I receive the premium and still own the stock. Selling covered calls is a relatively conservative options strategy that won't let me lose sleep (as long as I chose the correct underlying stock). I personally believe investors should master and use the covered call strategy, at least when they're first starting out.

Another suggestion: Check with your brokerage firm to see if you are allowed to sell covered calls in your 401(k) or IRA. Not only do you receive premium from selling covered calls in a tax-deferred plan, but you probably won't pay taxes on any short-term capital gains (always check with a tax advisor or the plan administrator to confirm). As long as you are aware of the risks, this strategy makes sense for many investors.

If you are determined to speculate with options, my belief is you should speculate 10 percent of the time with 10 percent of your money (although it ultimately depends on the individual). On occasion, a speculative opportunity comes along that you should pursue. It probably doesn't happen often, but when it does, you should be prepared to take advantage of it.

What are these opportunities? Sometimes they are hunches, perhaps a recommendation from a financial professional, or more than likely your own research. When you are ready to act, the options exchange will be there for you. To consistently make money as a speculator, however, you'll have to work hard. Although it's possible to be part of the minority that consistently makes money speculating in options, it's also not easy.

There are times you will want to purchase a stock but don't want to commit the capital. The options market allows you to make a relatively small investment with a chance at a large return. As long as you follow the "10-10 rule" (speculate 10 percent of the time with 10 percent of your money) and thoroughly research the underlying stock, your trading could be profitable and perhaps even hit that elusive home run once in a while.

Suggestion: Before you enter a position, plan for what could go wrong. That is why you must have rules for getting into a trade and rules for getting out. If your trade is not working out as you planned, cutting your losses is one of the smartest moves you can make.

One guideline is to close your position if you have more than a 6 or 7 percent loss. If you're not careful, your 7 percent loss could easily turn into a major loss. You must have valid fundamental and technical reasons (hope is not a reason) to hold the position. Otherwise, cut your losses at a predetermined percentage and look for another trade.

On the other hand, if your trade is working out as you planned, think about taking money off the table. One of the most important actions you can take is to protect your profits. By protecting profits, you'll have enough money to trade another day. As soon as your option becomes profitable, begin thinking of an exit point.

Don't forget that options have a funny way of expiring before you've made all your expected profits. There is an old but wise stock market rule: "Sell when you want to, not when you have to."

When I told Daniel, my friend who had made and lost $130,000 trading options in three days, that I was writing this book, he passed along this advice. "Tell your readers that if they are going to trade options, they better monitor their own account. You have to do what you think is right and not rely on anyone to tell you what to do." Good advice.

Before I go, I'd like to make three observations.

1. When trading, don't lose more money than you make (and if you consistently do, think about changing strategies).
2. It's not how much you make that's important, but how much you keep.
3. Finally, always remember that no one cares more about your money than you do (and believe me, I speak from experience).

Thank You

Thanks again for taking the time to read my book. I hope that I was able to teach you about options without making it confusing or boring. As I said in the beginning, my goal was to be the first person to write a book about options that actually made sense. Most important, if you can use what you learned in this book to make consistent profits or even a huge gain on occasion, then your time was well spent. (And I'd be really happy for you.) Good luck, and I wish you great success trading options.

If you have comments or questions about my book, feel free to send me an e-mail at msincere@gmail.com. In addition, if you notice any errors, please let me know so I can make corrections in the next edition. Finally, if you have time, feel free to stop by my Web site, www.michaelsincere.com. I hope to hear from you soon.

About the Author

After initially losing money in the stock market, **Michael Sincere** wrote his first book, *101 Investment Lessons from the Wizards of Wall Street* (Career Press, 1999). He interviewed some of the top traders and financial experts in the country to find out the lessons they had learned in the market so he could help others avoid the mistakes he made. This was followed by three more books, including *Understanding Stocks* (McGraw-Hill, 2003). This book has been so successful that McGraw-Hill turned it into the first of a series.

Sincere has written a number of columns and magazine articles on investing and trading. He has also been interviewed on dozens of national radio programs and has appeared on financial news programs such as CNBC and ABC's *World News Now!* to explain his trading strategies and talk about his books.

You can visit the author's Web site at http://www.michaelsincere. com.

Index